MYSTERIOUS PLACES

PETER UNDERWOOD
President of the Ghost Club

BOSSINEY BOOKS

For

LAURA

with love

First published in 1988
by Bossiney Books,
St Teath, Bodmin, Cornwall.

Typeset, printed and bound in
Great Britain by Penwell Limited,
Parkwood, Callington, Cornwall.

ISBN 0 948158 37 9

About the Author and the Book

Peter Underwood has been President of the Ghost Club (founded 1862) since 1960 and has probably heard more first-hand stories than any man alive. A long-standing member of The Society for Psychical Research, Vice-President of the Unitarian Society for Psychical Studies, a member of the Research Committee of the Psychic Research Organisation, he has lectured, written and broadcast extensively. He took part in the first official investigation into a haunting; has sat with physical and mental mediums and conducted investigations at séances; been present at exorcisms and regression; conducted world-wide tests in telepathy and extra-sensory perception; and has personally investigated scores of haunted houses.

He possesses comprehensive files of alleged hauntings in every county of the British Isles and many foreign countries, and his knowledge and experience has resulted in his being consulted on psychic and occult matters by the BBC and ITV.

Born at Letchworth Garden City in Hertfordshire, he now lives in a small village in Hampshire. He is Honorary Librarian of The Savage Club, 9 Fitzmaurice Place, Berkeley Square, London W1 where he can be contacted.

This is Peter Underwood's fifth title for Bossiney. In 1982 he produced *Ghosts of Devon,* an immediate bestseller for the cottage publishers, followed by *Ghosts of Cornwall* in 1983. In 1985 he made it an eerie hat-trick with *Ghosts of Somerset.* Then in 1986 came *Westcountry Hauntings:* a look at hauntings from Bristol down to Cornwall.

Now in *Mysterious Places* Peter Underwood, Britain's No. 1 Ghost Hunter, writes of locations that 'seem to have been touched by a magic hand'. He visits places as different as the haunted old prison at Bodmin in Cornwall and a farm at Winkleigh in Devon where a strange three-way agricultural suicide took place in 1975. He looks, too, at ancient stone circles and investigates strange happenings in the New Forest. Words and photographs and drawings all manage to convey 'something of the mystery and the magic' of this eerie expedition.

By the same author

The Ghost Hunter's Guide
This Haunted Isle
Queen Victoria's Other World
Dictionary of the Supernatural
The Ghost Hunters
Haunted London
Into the Occult
Deeper into the Occult
Gazetteer of British Ghosts
Gazetteer of Scottish and Irish Ghosts
Ghosts of Wales
Hauntings: New Light on Ten Famous Cases
A Host of Hauntings
The Vampire's Bedside Companion
Complete Book of Dowsing and Divining
Ghosts of North West England
A Ghost Hunter's Handbook
Ghosts of Hampshire and the Isle of Wight
Ghosts of Devon
Ghosts of Cornwall
Ghosts of Somerset
Ghosts of Kent
Westcountry Hauntings
Horror Man—The Life of Boris Karloff
Life's a Drag—A Life of Danny La Rue
Lives to Remember: A Case Book on Reincarnation
(with Leonard Wilder)
The Ghosts of Borley: a critical history of 'the most haunted
house in England' (with Dr Paul Tabori)
No Common Task—The Autobiography of a Ghost Hunter
Jack the Ripper—One Hundred Years of Mystery

As Editor: Thirteen Famous Ghost Stories, Everyman's Library

Acknowledgements

The author wishes to express his gratitude and appreciation for the help he has received from Anthea Barker, Dr John Beloff, Paul Broadhurst, Mrs Pauline Clare, Rosemary Clinch, Judy Housley, Marilyn and Trevor Kenward, Barbara and Duncan McKenzie, Miss Nell St John Montague, Colonel Cecil Powney CBE, Mrs Doris Pullen, Margaret Royal, Dick Sheppard, Frank Thorne, Margot Towell, his publisher Michael Williams, the staff at Alresford, Okehampton and other Public Libraries, his wife Joyce Elizabeth and also his correspondents, many of whom wish to remain unidentified but he is enormously grateful to them for sending him details of their experiences.

Plate Acknowledgements

Front Cover by Ray Bishop
Drawings by Felicity Young
Ray Bishop: pages 6, 7, 30, 32, 34, 35, 54, 59, 66, 70, 91
Richard Isbell: pages 8, 33, 72, 73, 74
Rosemary Clinch: pages 28, 48, 50, 77, 78
Julia Davey: pages 9, 39, 101
Trevor Kenward: pages 62, 63
Maggie Ginger: pages 95, 96, 100
Paul Honeywill: page 44
Ken Duxbury: page 68
Studio St. Ives: page 89

Introduction

The secrets of Britain lie in its mysterious places.

In practically every part of the British Isles there are granite monoliths, stone circles and odd places: an eerie atmosphere, perhaps, a sense of unease, a feeling that some force or power is in command. Such impressions are by no means uncommon and I am always receiving letters recounting some strange happening, unreal and unforgettable—unlike anything else ever experienced. These letters come from people in all walks of life and from every part of these islands but I have long noticed that a great many come from

RIGHT: *Water often travels through mysterious places. Golitha Falls on a November morning.*

BELOW: *The Hurlers on Bodmin Moor: Living stones that have fascinated mankind for centuries.*

the Westcountry, that magic land that only with reluctance yields up its secrets; a land that is full of legends and old beliefs, of witchcraft and ghost-ridden properties, of reputed visits by King Arthur and by the Devil himself; but above all it is a land of living stones with strange powers.

In this look at some of the truly mysterious places I have tried to ring the changes. I have included not only some of the stories and experiences pertaining to those living stones that have fascinated mankind for thousands of years, but I have also looked at some of the other places where whole series of apparently inexplicable, incomprehensible happenings have occurred and these are the places that affect some people in mysterious ways.

Travelling with an open mind some parts do seem to have been touched by a magic hand, where the inexplicable and the all-powerful can still be encountered, usually suddenly and unexpectedly, but unmistakably with the knowledge that here is something not of this world; something that is above and beyond the everyday reality; something that is mysterious. We live in a very mysterious world if only we have the awareness to appreciate it.

Peter Underwood

The Savage Club
Berkeley Square
London W1

LEFT: *The Cheesewring which stands on the great ley line of the West.*

BELOW: *Woods, too, belong to mysterious Britain: 'some parts do seem to have been touched by a magic hand.'*

Mysterious Places

Bodmin, Cornwall

The old prison at Bodmin was built in 1778 when the jail at Launceston Castle was no longer acceptable; it was enlarged in the early 1820s and became the only county jail in 1837 when the new Assizes Hall was built in the town. It was later taken over by the Naval authorities who continued to use it until about 1919 when it was put up for sale. In World War One some of the nation's valuables were stored there and during the Second World War it was used as a Civil Defence base and then by the American forces as a barracks.

Prisoners were hanged at Bodmin Jail for such varied, and in some cases such petty, crimes as burglary, stealing three sheep or an ewe, highway robbery, stealing a watch, killing a mare, forgery and setting fire to a corn rick, as well as more justifiably for the crime of murder. One of the murderers hanged here was Matthew Weeks who killed his sweetheart Charlotte Dymond. Her ghost still walks the long green slopes below Roughtor on Bodmin Moor where she met her end. Bodmin Old Prison was in fact 'the last place on earth' for over fifty men and women.

Much of the building remains little changed today and some visitors in recent years have reported hearing the rattle of keys in the vicinity of the cells; a common enough sound in the old days. Other visitors have heard heavy footsteps near one of the old archways, for which there appears to be no prosaic explanation.

All the actual hangings, except four, were carried out in public, outside the jail walls, and here too a number of people have reported an overwhelming feeling of remorse and sadness, of grief and des-

RIGHT: *The old prison at Bodmin: a haunted, haunting place.*

pair—almost as though some remnant of the happenings here have become impressed upon the atmosphere, to be picked up on occasions by perceptive people. This feeling of depression and utter despondency is perhaps most apparent in the towering old cell blocks where once some two hundred prisoners lived out their sentences. These cell blocks have been left to rot and plants and birds and rats are now the only living things in this place of desolation.

Here, countless prisoners spent months and sometimes years picking oakum—pulling to pieces old rope for remaking—and even tombstone engraving. The death knell was sounded on execution days from the centre of the jail, the forty-foot-high tower, a vantage point for warders to look down on all parts of the ominous old building.

In more recent times the premises have been used as a dance hall and a night club. Carole and Emryn Lewis have many stories to tell of the time they lived here, stories of strange happenings, often trivial in themselves but seemingly inexplicable. They became convinced that the place was haunted.

From time to time their television set would play up and it seemed to be affected by outside forces as technicians could never find any fault; and when the Lewis family went away for a few days 'things mysteriously went wrong'. Objects went missing and would eventually be found in some place that had already been most carefully searched. Nor were Carole and Emryn Lewis the only people to report such happenings. Previous managers had complained of 'moving' plates and of dogs refusing to go near some of the old parts of the prison.

Sometimes Emryn Lewis had the distinct impression that he was being followed by someone or something invisible as he traversed the doom-laden old jail and even today, in broad daylight, it is not difficult to imagine haunted eyes following you as you move about this silent, cold and distinctly unwelcoming place.

Once Carole Lewis definitely heard voices when there was no-one but herself in the building; another time she heard a man's cough which could not have had a natural origin. 'Time after time' she said she would hear something, look round and discover there was no-one

RIGHT: *President of the Ghost Club, Peter Underwood. This is his fifth title for Bossiney.*

in the building, 'at least no living person. Quite simply there was nothing to account for what I heard . . .' she asserted.

To her and to her husband and to many people before and after them, Bodmin Jail is a haunted place.

Budleigh Salterton, Devon

In 1981 the titled widow of a former university professor wrote to me regarding a certain ghost which I had mentioned briefly in one of my books. I was able to supply her with chapter and verse concerning that particular case and she was then kind enough to relate a most interesting personal experience. I cannot do better than quote from her letter, altering only slightly certain passages to avoid identification.

'As you may have surmised I did have a deeper reason for my enquiry. I lost my husband a few years ago and was staggered when mentioning this to a local businessman, from whom I was getting some supplies, to have him accuse me of pulling his leg! He's a very nice chap, very extrovert, and having built up a flourishing business in a time of economic depression, a good businessman and nobody's fool. But he took a great deal of convincing of my husband's demise for he said he had been saying "Good Morning" to him at least twice a week for the last three months. When I said it must have been somebody else who looked a bit like him, he wouldn't have this either: "I *know* your husband," he said. "I go past your house four times a day and in the past he's been in here too, getting stuff for you . . ."

'Obviously he must have met him face to face—you don't greet somebody when looking at the back of his head. Finally I pointed out that I'd met his (the businessman's) wife in the village shop soon after my husband died and had told her I'd got to go a long way to a Memorial Service and I wasn't fancying it: whereupon he said, "Yes, I do remember, now; and what do you think I said? Funny, the things you find out when someone dies. I always thought the man who lived with her in that house *was* her husband, but he can't be, because I saw him this morning!" Alas, I have no witness, and I hadn't the heart to accuse him of pulling my leg! He looked so shattered when I finally convinced him, I'm sure he believed what he'd said he's seen.

'Some months later my stepson was here and I told him about it; and then when I happened to meet the businessman again I asked him whether he could add anything to the story and he told me that from the day he told me about it and I had told him my husband was dead, he had never seen the figure again—and he'd looked. Incidentally, there can't be many spooks who've led the neighbours to make compromising speculations about their widows! If he is around, or somewhere (and as a Christian I believe he must be, in some form) I should think he's having a good laugh. And he's a wonderful ghost to have—long may he haunt me!'

Perhaps there is something strange about the streets of Budleigh Salterton for I have several reports of unidentified ghosts being encountered here including one incident where a resident was tending her garden when she noticed a perfect stranger walking towards her. He was only remarkable because he was dressed in a black jacket and striped trousers and wearing a bowler hat; absolutely out of place in a country lane. As he walked quickly past, my correspondent realised that she had heard no sound of footsteps, in fact no sound of any kind. Hurriedly she looked up the road but there was no sign of the mysterious stranger, no car in sight, nothing . . . but that she had seen the man she was absolutely sure.

Another correspondent tells me that she was walking down a road in Budleigh Salterton when she saw a couple coming towards her. They seemed to be in animated conversation but as they passed no sound reached her ears. A second after they had passed she looked round, mildly puzzled, and she was astounded to find the road completely empty. There was nowhere the couple could have turned off and in any case there was simply no time. Later she heard that other people had seen the same couple in the same place but who they were or why they appear is anybody's guess.

Carn Euny and other Cornish Fogous

Not far from Sancreed, three miles west of Penzance, is the ancient settlement of Carn Euny. It lies north of the Blind Fiddler, that

solitary monolith, ten feet tall, that is supposed to be the petrified figure of a fiddler who was turned to stone for making music on a sacred day. It cannot but be interesting that all standing stones share the same legend in local folklore: they are the petrified remains of people punished for playing or dancing on forbidden days.

Here, at Carn Euny, there is an impressive fogou which could well be an ancient storage place for occult energy. All the Cornish fogous have long been regarded as fairy dwellings and are thought to have originally been situated underneath the threshold of a human's house or sometimes under the hearthstone; the hearthstone serving as the door. There is a Scottish tale of cakes being baked and disappearing, thought to have been taken by the fairies, and in one tale, when the hearthstone is raised, a tiny hand comes up to snatch another cake!

Whatever the origin of these fogous they are stone-built galleries with a slab roof below ground level and date back two thousand years. They are almost certainly strange cellars of some kind but the curious experiences reported by many visitors suggest that what may have have been stored there was no prosaic substance.

The courtyard houses of Carn Euny can be classified as a prehistoric village of the Iron Age, but the Department of the Environment state in their pamphlet that this village is 'one of an enigmatic group of monuments found in southwest Cornwall'. A semi-underground structure, the fogou is set in a deep tunnel leading to a round chamber. Once built it could well have been used for many different purposes over the centuries, 'but its original purpose still evades us and it remains one of the most remarkable prehistoric monuments in the country'.

Could these fogous—there is another at Halligye eight miles north-west of Lizard Point—have once been infused with magic that would enhance the survival chances of the soul and even the mortal remains of ancient man after death? Were these places the sites of evil ceremonies? At the Boleigh fogou at St Buryan the devil himself was supposed to play his pipe to witches who held their sabbat

LEFT: *The Blind Fiddler, that solitary monolith, said to be the petrified figure of the fiddler.*

there; afterwards the witches would assume the forms of hares and run into the fogou. Could they, as Evelyn Clark asks in her detailed record *Cornish Fogous* (Methuen, 1961), have been built to satisfy some primitive urge and fundamental instinct of the periods from which they originate; to store, to inhabit, even to worship, below ground? Or could they have been erected for some forgotten way of concentrating earth energies—or even for shamanistic initiatory practices, as suggested by Janet and Colin Bord in their *Ancient Mysteries of Britain* (Grafton, 1986)?

I have in my possession several reports from people who have visited these lonely and deserted places and felt, overwhelmingly, that they were no longer alone. Invisible eyes seemed to watch them as they entered these strange places. Some are certain their minds and intellects were tampered with in some indefinable way so that they felt out of control and were glad to stumble back into daylight and normality. Others have thought they glimpsed vague shapes and forms that seemed to hurry away as they entered and still others have experienced a strange affinity with these places and believe that they have somehow been there before, many centuries earlier.

Writing of fogous some fifty years ago S.P.B. Mais said, 'the man who fails to be moved by these eerie relics of a bygone age . . . is to be pitied. Cornwall speaks to him in vain.' If my records suggest anything, they suggest that for some people Cornwall does not speak in vain and, for some, the Cornish fogous leave a lasting and somewhat disturbing impression that never disappears.

Cerne Abbas, Dorset and other Hill Figures

Perhaps the most remarkable and astonishing of all Britain's various hill figures, if only for its unashamed sexual attributes, the Cerne Abbas Giant, 180 feet high and 44 feet across the shoulder,

RIGHT: *The Fogou at Carn Euny: an ancient settlement in the Hundred of Penwith.*

Felicity Young.

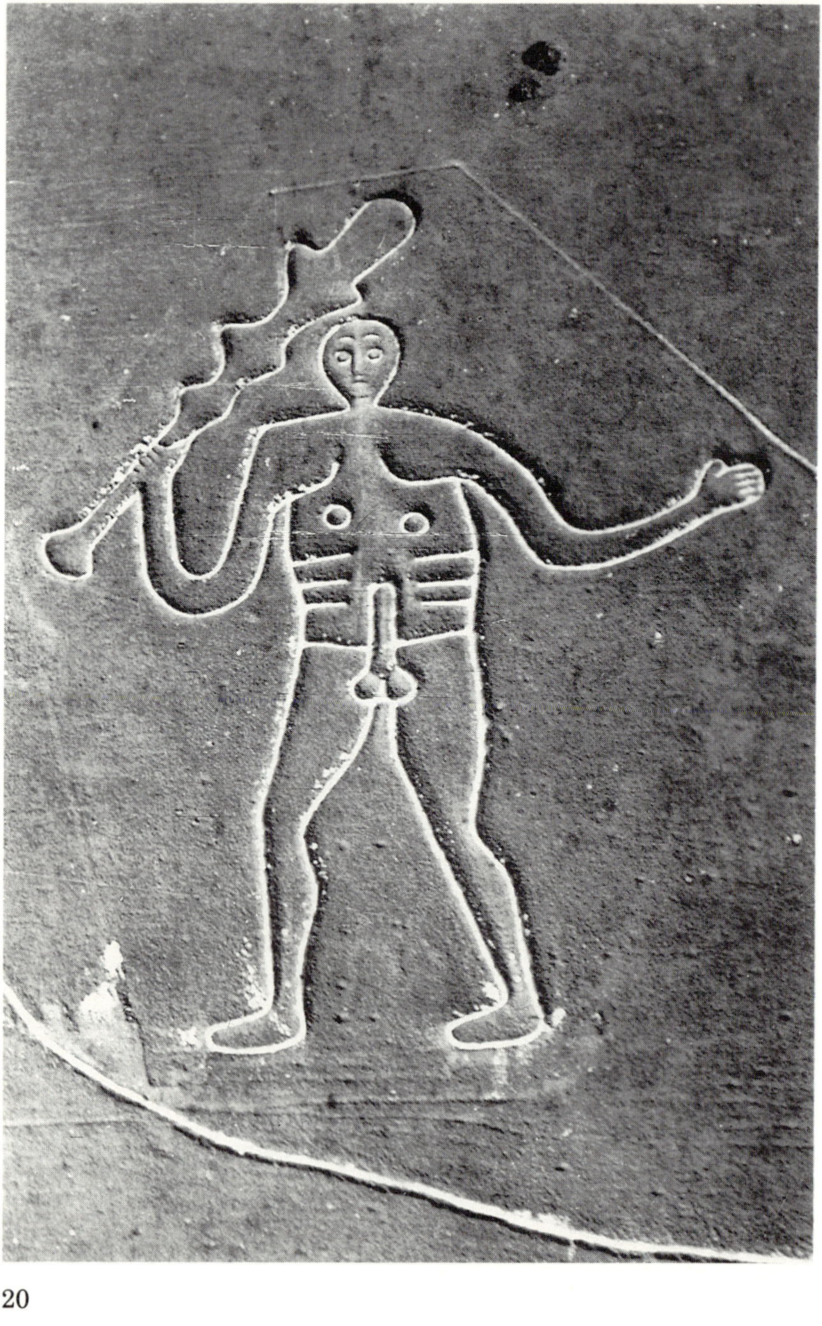

would appear to be a fertility symbol of some kind and indeed it has been used as such within living memory. It is a striking figure: one arm is outstretched and a knobbly, crab-like club is held aloft in the other hand; the formidable figure is stepping across the countryside and looking straight ahead but it is its 30 foot long erect phallus and anatomically correct giant testicles that make it unique.

Other ancient and spectacular hill figures still in existence include the Long Man of Wilmington in East Sussex and the White Horses at Uffington in Berkshire and at Westbury in Wiltshire and it is by no means unlikely that other hill figures await discovery.

The Uffington White Horse has a stylised outline that resembles a dragon as much as a horse and an adjoining mound is known as Dragon Hill. Interestingly, legend has it that it was here that St George slew a dragon and the two bare patches of ground on which no turf will grow are supposed to mark the spot where dragon's blood was spilled. An age-old superstition maintained that to stand in the eye of the figure and revolve three times ensured the success of any wish.

The Westbury White Horse is something of a mystery but it is generally supposed to replace an earlier version which may have been cut to celebrate King Alfred's victory over the Danes. On the other hand no record has been discovered of its existence before the eighteenth century when the Reverend Francis Wise wrote that it had 'been wrought within living memory'. Yet, in common with all the early hill figures the Westbury White Horse adjoins ancient earthworks which were in all probability sacred enclosures where fertility rites of some kind were carried out and these were almost certainly the forerunners and the origins of many of the ancient fairs and festivals celebrated in villages today.

The monstrous Cerne Abbas Giant is carved on the steep slope of Trundle, Trendle or Frying Pan Hill, names which also apply to the Iron Age camp or fort. One is reminded of the curious eminence by Goodwood racecourse in Sussex, beneath which a golden calf is said to lie buried. A quarter of a mile south is Cerne Abbas Church, which was probably erected in the vicinity of the giant purposely and in line with Pope Gregory the Great's advice to St Augustine in the sixth century to take over heathen temples and shrines to en-

LEFT: *The Cerne Abbas Giant*

courage people to keep coming to their familiar places of worship. One example is the monks of Lanercost who, in 1268, made a fertility figure of Priapus for the local people whose cattle were diseased.

Who the Cerne Giant represents is still unknown: it could be a Hercules figure—his emblem was a club—and he was also regarded as a god of fertility; possibly it represents the gods Helith or Corinaeus, both once worshipped in the district; or Helios the Greek sun god, perhaps representing a pagan cult of the sun with attendant fertility rites, centred on Cerne; could it have originated in the colourful story of local people finding a real sheep-eating giant asleep on the hillside and having killed him on the spot they drew his outline to mark the event? Or did the abbot or monks at the nearby abbey create the figure as a satirical joke at the time of the dissolution of the monasteries? This could explain why the figure has never been defaced or obliterated.

What is certain is that fertility has always been associated with the Cerne Giant, or 'His Mightiness' as he is known locally. Well within living memory women who wish to conceive have sat on the great phallus at midnight; other childless couples have slept there to improve their chances and not a few have performed the act of love there to give full effect to the charm. Such activities may well have been a natural progression from the maypole dancing and other festivals that were once regularly carried out in the rectangular 'frying pan' above the Giant and are still said to continue around midsummer. The maypole itself is a sophisticated representation of the phallus.

In the 1968 edition of *The Giant of Cerne Abbas,* West Country Folklore Monographs, H.S.L. Dewar says: '. . . it is quite impossible to live in the district and be unaware that not only young girls who fear to lose their boyfriends, are in the habit of visiting the figure and perambulating his frame, perhaps with a giggle and hand-in-hand with a girl friend, but grown women as well who fear to lose their mates. Women about to get married, too, as has been told me personally by their husbands in later life, used to look on it as not only a normal and respectable act, but the duty of common sense to visit the Giant to express their hopes during the week prior to marriage. Some of my friends tell me also that women of their acquaintance confess to having sat on the appropriate portions of the erstwhile god to assure themselves of the future.'

Colourful explanations for the Giant include the idea that he is the representation of a giant who ate babies—Thomas Hardy is among those who heard this story; and something to do with Julius Caesar's Druidic sacrifice, the huge wickerwork figure packed with living people and set ablaze—this would have been a terrible but spectacular sight indeed were it carried out in the vicinity of the Cerne Giant and such an act would have provided another reason for the rectangular earthwork above the Giant's head: the Trendle could have been a palisaded enclosure where victims were herded to await sacrifice.

The Celtic festival that welcomed Spring was called Beltane from the Gaelic for 'blaze-fire' and Spring is the season of fertility; so the most obvious attributes of the Giant and the time when the ancient hillside might be expected to pulsate and become alive again may represent an age-old fertility rite that is now lost in the mists of time.

Curiously the only reports in my possession of anything of a ghostly nature taking place in the vicinity of the Cerne Abbas Giant are all in springtime. Most frequent are overwhelming but invisible impressions of some maleficent presence. There are, too, several reports of a gigantic 'shadow' being glimpsed and, just for a moment, an awful feeling of doom and despair. Can such impressions and experiences be deep-seated folk memories of past happenings in the immediate vicinity of the mysterious Cerne Abbas Giant?

Chysauster, near Penzance, Cornwall

Nearby, north off the road towards Newmill, stands one of the best-known of Britain's Iron Age villages, Chysauster, which may well have once been a prehistoric 'university' inhabited by astronomers and geomancers of a past age; for as at Carn Euny, the underground chamber, or fogou, may have been a sort of storage place for some form of built-up cosmic energy.

Interestingly enough official archaeological opinion avers there is little evidence of any industry in the area, so-called 'mixed farming'

Two aspects of Chysauster captured by Tintagel painter Felicity Young. This is one of Britain's best known Iron Age villages.

being the only suggested means by which the one-time inhabitants of Chysauster could have made a living.

Jacquetta Hawkes has pointed out that the architecture of Chysauster is strangely Mediterranean and she speculates that the people who lived there may have mined ore which they shipped from St Michael's Mount across to the Continent, thereby making the link with Mediterranean countries that seems evident.

Several of the dwelling houses can be entered and each has a central courtyard with small rooms off where domestic rubbish and pottery has been found. The houses are complete with hearths and drains, workrooms and cattle-sheds. Each house had, and in some cases still has, a terraced garden with a low stone wall and it has

been established that terraced fields once stood on a nearby hill-slope. The occupiers of Chysauster may have been farmers but if so they were prosperous farmers and their income was supplemented by an early form of industry, almost certainly tin-working, for a trench is still discernible leading from the settlement to a stream where tin working was certainly carried out.

Chysauster has a very strange atmosphere. On each visit I have felt distinctly aware of 'something' from long ago still hovering about the place and I have quite a number, the best part of a dozen, independent reports from visitors who have been aware of something odd, sometimes a little sinister, and always invisible but unmistakable about Chysauster.

Clevedon, Somerset

In a small cave beside the Bristol Channel there is the stone face of a one-eyed god carved in the rocks. It may be the head of Bran the Blessed, guardian of the coast, or the goddess Nemet—she of the Groves, or in fact almost any other Celtic god, for the carving at Ladye Bay has always been surrounded by mystery.

The head is deeply etched in the hard stone of a sloping boulder and lies in a little chamber under a pile of enormous fallen rocks, some of them weighing many tons, boulders that must at some time in the far past have fallen to the beach as the cliff collapsed. It is the only one of its kind in the South West and has been estimated by archaeological experts to be about two thousand years old. In an area thickly covered with Celtic settlements the idea that the head is the work of a schoolboy or a man trapped by the tide in 1910, as has been suggested, seems most unlikely. Then there is the theory that it depicts the face of an alien invader from Mars. American reports in 1948 and a photograph taken in 1976 suggest that a mile-wide rock in the Cydonia region of Mars is carved in the semblance of a human-type face but showing a left eye socket, one pupil, one eyeball and a continuation of hair around the forehead—exactly like the Ladye Bay head.

The face is only about the size of the palm of the hand and is surrounded by a deeply-cut, oval channel. It probably represents a severed head or a *tête coupée* similar to those found in France and Ireland.

The one closed eye may express the dark, evil side of nature, while the open eye represents the bright and beneficial side of the deity. Can it be Nemetona or Nemet, The Hag, the forest deity who was feared and whose dark side was far better known than the other side?

But if it is Bran the Blessed then it is something very different. Bran crossed to this country from Ireland and was a beneficial deity. When he felt his end approaching he ordered that after death

RIGHT: *The stone face of a one-eyed god carved in rock alongside the Bristol Channel.*

Ladye Bay.

his head should be severed from his body and, following the flight of his sacred ravens, the head was to be buried where the birds settled.

Legend has it that the ravens led Bran's followers to what is now Tower Hill in London and that the head of Bran was buried there. He had promised to lay undisturbed as long as his ravens continued to live nearby and, what was more, an additional advantage would be that the country would be safe from its enemies. Excepting the Norman Conquest the forecast seems to have been fulfilled and there are still ravens at the Tower of London where they are carefully fed and jealously guarded.

But why should a representation of Bran have been made in a lonely spot by the sea? Bran was also known as The Protector and his face may well have been carved where it was likely to repel invaders sailing up the Bristol Channel. It could be one of many sacred carvings which have disappeared over the centuries. There is a second face cut into the cliff not far from Ladye Cave but being in the open it has attracted vandals over the years and has been deliberately defaced.

The immediate countryside is rich in ancient history. Less than a mile away there is the quaintly-named Walton-in-Gordano and a hill above the village has revealed evidence of a large camp occupied from Neolithic times until the late Iron Age. 'Walton' has been translated as meaning 'the place of the stranger' or 'foreigner'. Only five miles away, at Yatton, a temple of the Roman period has been discovered but of the gods worshipped there nothing is known.

Possibly the mysterious face in Ladye Bay is the sole surviving part of a secret shrine where ancient people who disapproved of the new temple and its strange gods gathered to honour and pray to the more ancient deities revered by their fathers and grandfathers.

The spot where the face in the rock lies is very difficult to reach. It involves a dangerous climb down the cliff and a risky scramble among the boulders. The small cave has only two entrances: one is a narrow opening overlooking the sea, where light falls upon the face; the other is a short but steep tunnel leading from the cliff into the back of the chamber.

Everyone who should know agrees that the face is very ancient and almost certainly Celtic; it is nearly as fresh and sharply defined as when it was cut perhaps two thousand years ago—yet its origin, its meaning, its significance and its influence is completely unknown.

Commonmoor, near St Cleer, Liskeard, Cornwall

I am indebted to a correspondent, Mrs Doris Pullen of Havant, for alerting me to the fact that the area around the village of Commonmoor seems to be a mysterious place on occasions. Mrs Pullen tells me that as a child one of her weekly chores was a Saturday walk from Commonmoor to St Cleer with radio accumulators for charging.

St CLEER HOLY WELL
RESTORED 1864

Since time immemorial St Cleer has had an annual ceremony on St John's Eve, 23 June, of 'banishing the witches' which in years past consisted of crowning a bonfire with a witch's broom and hat while a sickle with a handle of newly cut oak was thrown into the flames. Sometimes herbs were cast into the fire but more often wreaths of St John's wort would be hung about the village, a traditional safeguard against witchcraft.

Mrs Pullen knew the district well: she always walked to school each day and in her spare hours, on Sundays and weekday evenings, she would stroll across the moors, always alone and completely unafraid—something that could not be recommended in this enlightened age.

In 1931, when she was nine years old, one beautiful, warm, still and very clear day, she was ambling along the road bordering the moor when she chanced to glance at a rock which was perhaps twenty-five feet away from her. There she saw, as plain as daylight, the face of a pretty young woman peering out at her from behind the rock, the long, blonde, wavy hair floating in the breeze—which was very strange for there was not a breath or hint of a breeze that could keep the hair suspended.

Young Doris stared at the odd sight, watching it as she passed until it was no longer in her view; she had no thought of fear or of anything supernatural and, although she was rather surprised at what she saw, it didn't enter her mind to approach the rock or even to cross the road to look closer at the face and the floating hair.

It is the only experience of its kind she ever had but, she tells me, 'the scene is as vivid today as it was on the day I saw it and although we left Cornwall the following year, I'm sure I could lead you straight to that rock. What *did* I see?'

St Cleer has an old holy well, one of Cornwall's many secret shrines where natural springs bubble to the surface and become famous for miraculous healings, powers of prophecy, magical properties or as some sort of threshold to other realms. Paul Broadhurst has made a study of the two hundred holy wells in Cornwall and the Scillies and his impressive volume *Secret Shrines* (published by the author from Trebeath, Egloskerry, Launceston, 1988) details

LEFT: *Ancient wells have a reputation for healing power. Here is the well at St Cleer on the edge of Bodmin Moor.*

ABOVE: *King Doniert Stone near St Cleer.*
RIGHT: *Daniel Gumb's Cave below the Cheesewring.*

the histories, lore, legends and literature of these fascinating old wells. He finds these places truly timeless with almost living spirits that affect all but the most prosaic of mankind. The impressive well at St Cleer is no exception and was in particular renowned for its healing qualities. At one time, on almost any day, the lame and the blind and the crippled, adults and children, would flock for relief and not a few claimed to be completely cured. The St Cleer bowser or ducking well was once used in attempts to cure lunacy and epilepsy. There was and perhaps still is 'something' in the air in this part of Cornwall.

A nearby vicarage was supposed to be 'haunted' by the reincarnated form of a previous vicar, Parson Jupp, and the servants were always careful never to kill a spider in the house for it was believed that it was in this form that the former master of the house returned.

Not far away are King Doniert's Stone, the puzzling Cheesewring

Golitha Falls in winter.

and the impressive but ominous and melancholy Golitha Falls. King Doniert, or Dumgarth, was a King of Cornwall who was drowned in or about the year 878. The Cheesewring is a very odd shape with smaller stones at the bottom, spreading into a bulbous middle and then smaller stones again at the top. At least one quarryman was convinced that it was the result and a relic of the Biblical Deluge while others have remarked on the peaceful atmosphere only occasionally broken by unexplained sounds that are so weird and unnatural that they defy explanation.

Below the Cheesewring is Daniel Gumb's cave. He was a stone cutter and amateur mathematician who lived the life of a hermit here until his death in 1776. His chiselled diagrams are still extant

Does King Doniert haunt these woods?

on the huge stone slab which formed the roof of his cavern.

The Cheesewring was indisputably once a witch's initiation rock and the top stone is still said to turn when it hears a cock crow. This very odd place may once have been the home of an ancient Druid who possessed a cup made of gold, the contents of which were inexhaustible; a cup that was stolen and is reputedly buried hereabouts. Or was it the gold cup found in 1818 when a nearby cairn, known as King Arthur's Grave, was excavated; a ribbed cup that was dated by experts circa 1500 BC and now resides in the British Museum? The Cheesewring is said to be on a ley line that runs from St Michael's Mount, passes through Glastonbury Tor and ends on the east coast near Lowestoft.

Exmoor, Somerset

One of the more recent ghost reports that I have received concerns a farmhouse on the edge of Exmoor. Because there is still the possibility of investigation I am not disclosing the exact whereabouts of the property or the real names of the people concerned but every other particular is factual.

I first heard of the case from a correspondent who was kind enough to write to me following a visit to the house. He writes: 'I am sixty-two and have always favoured the view of most serious parapsychologists that there is a rational explanation for most apparently psychic experiences. So I wonder if you can set my mind at rest and give me a possible explanation of what I am about to relate—as briefly as I can.

'I arrived at the farm late on Thursday evening last, having driven down from London with the owner, Mr "Willis", to attend a function his wife had organised to raise funds for a village charity. A house of some kind has been on the site for probably five or six hundred years. The previous owner had lived in the house for many years and had made no structural alterations and had never had any odd experiences. The present occupants moved in about a year ago and have already made extensive alterations. The farm is enclosed by hills and there is a stream close by. Many years ago the track to the house was a minor road leading elsewhere. Now it is a dead end.

'I went to bed about half an hour after midnight, my room being in the oldest and least altered part of the house; possibly once a cottage dating from Elizabethan times for it is possible that the other rooms of the present house were built on to this cottage. The central heating is excellent. I was warm under a thick duvet. Then I became very cold down to my waist. I thought I must have a chill coming on from faulty air-conditioning in my London office. I got up and put on a dressing gown. Then, with my arms almost frozen, I had to wind a woollen shawl round them to get any warmth . . . I began to be angry with myself; I had a cold sweat and couldn't sleep and it was a bad start to my holiday.

'Then I heard a click, exactly as if a radio set had been turned on and immediately it seemed to me a programme came on: five or six adult voices talking quietly together, in gentle, almost soothing tones. Not a radio play, too restrained and lacking any sense of drama; more like a family sitting round a table for an unimportant discussion. After about two minutes—click, the radio was switched off and the atmosphere felt empty momentarily, just as when a radio is switched off. I thought Mr Willis must have left his radio alarm on in his dressing room to my left, a room away. I thought nothing more of it and gradually I became warmed and dozed but only slept in snatches. (When the radio switched off I got up and went to the lavatory; Mr Willis was awake and next day he told me he had heard me and it was 1.30 a.m.)

'The two window curtains in my room were open; it was dark and I glanced at my watch just before 4 a.m. I lay half-asleep and then, click, the broadcast came on again, an exact repetition of the first time. Two minutes, then click and off. I thought to myself I was obviously a bit feverish with a chill, but how odd that I should half-dream a repetition of the earlier incident. I was only upset because I was sleeping so badly and would be tired next day.

'Next day the plan had been to rush out and do some shopping but when I was called for breakfast I was so tired I opted to stay in bed for a couple of hours. The Willis's drove off at 9.20 a.m. My room was in full daylight and I am sure I was not asleep, just relaxing when—click—the radio came on with exactly the same discussion as before. I was amazed but told myself it was because I was trying to sleep in the daytime and was in one of those feverish states when you have half-dreams, yet I thought it was quite bizarre, my mind turning out again and again the same experiences. I dozed uneasily and some time later—click—the whole scenario again. This time I listened more closely (previously I had taken it as dream nonsense) and this time I distinguished someone speaking of "Uncle Gus" or of "Gussie" and a female voice said something about "don't tell Aunt Emmie (or Emma or maybe just Emmie) on the way to the church". I had the impression they were all talking together in subdued voices, maybe trying to soothe someone. There was no drama, no excitement, I felt as if I was overhearing snatches of a discussion which had absolutely nothing to do with me. In its quiet style I thought it was a little like a family talk on occasions when I was a child. There were only adult voices and with no distinctive accents, just ordinary quiet talk.

'As soon as the sounds clicked off, I roused myself, told myself it was stupid to lie there having odd dreams, better get up, have a bath and buck up. I did so and found it was about 11 a.m. The Willis's arrived back and jokingly I told Mr Willis I'd had a spooky experience . . . though that wasn't really what I meant. I meant a bizarre one, due to being feverish. He immediately said, "Did you see the jug levitate, as 'Mary' did?" Mary is his wife. Just then Mary came in. "No," I said. "I just kept hearing a radio programme." Mary interrupted me, saying, "Quiet voices, all talking together, for a couple of minutes, then clicking off?" We each elaborated on what we had heard and she said she had heard it about a dozen times, about once a week, and usually very soon after she had gone to bed, and was still awake. She always was taken by surprise and found herself leaning over to switch off the radio near the bed, then realising that it was not switched on. Always it was the same group discussion. It seemed to come from a short distance away, to her left; just as mine did. She said it sounded like adults gathered together for a wake, quietly soothing someone. And I then realised that this is just what it did sound like. We could think of no other type of conversation that was so appropriate. She had not mentioned it to her husband because he is deaf and she felt sure he would not hear the soft click of the radio or the voices, and he had heard nothing.

'We felt it was not a radio broadcast because it was repeated so often and it was of no dramatic significance. It could not be conversation drifting to us from somewhere outside since again it was repeated so often, day and night. There is no tape recording apparatus in the house or anything that could have been activated. I am a matter-of-fact sort of person who has no reason to make a drama out of a spooky incident; my life is quite interesting enough without that!

'I haven't written about Mary's other experience: a jug of milk levitating and emptying itself over her oven top before smashing to pieces—and this happened while her two dogs were cheerfully sitting in the kitchen and she was just entering by the other door, to let them into the garden. This was her only other odd experience and seems to me to be unconnected with our shared one. On the remaining two nights that I was at the farm I heard nothing, slept uneasily, but did not have a chill!'

I wrote to Mrs Willis asking about the possibility of a few Ghost Club members spending a night in the 'most haunted room' and attempting to record the mysterious voices. Mrs Willis said she

Exmoor has a lonely and sometimes Supernatural quality.

would be very pleased for us to carry out any investigation but they could not accommodate an overnight stay; they would be delighted for us to spend a day with them; however since the voices had mostly been reported outside the hours of daylight, it was decided to await further developments before conducting any investigation. In reply to my enquiry as to her personal experiences Mrs Willis wrote:

'The conversation that I heard was identical to that heard by our friend. It occurred at 11 p.m. in the master bedroom built about forty years ago. It has been repeated several times but always late at night. It doesn't seem to have any regularity or pattern. I haven't heard anything for a few months now. Our friend who wrote to you heard his two episodes in the guest room at 2.30 a.m. and 4.30 a.m., this is part of the old area of the house, and again at 9.30 a.m. and 10.30 a.m.

'There is, however, something else that has happened to me repeatedly. When we originally bought the farmhouse we selected it because it has a friendly, welcoming feeling, unlike some of the other properties we viewed. We moved into the house in the July and all was well. After our friend's experience I was alone in the kitchen one December, around two o'clock in the morning hanging Christmas cards around the room. I am a very methodical and intense person and I was concentrating very hard on colour and design to achieve the effect I wanted. I was very involved in this activity and it was around 3 a.m. when I felt something foreign in my presence. I didn't see anything or hear anything. I just felt an overwhelming presence that was very frightening. We have a very large "L" shaped kitchen/breakfast room and this presence seemed to be situated near the original back door.

'I became so frightened that I summoned my two dogs, who were asleep, and ran up to bed leaving the cards, blue-tac, scissors, etc., and the lights on. The next night I resumed my Christmas card activity with no interruption and the night passed very pleasantly. The third night I again felt something foreign to be near the back door and I did not enter that area during my middle-of-the-night activities.

'Several weeks passed and no unusual happenings occurred. In the February I was sitting at the breakfast room table about 2.30 a.m. reading the newspaper when an overwhelming presence made itself felt very near to where I was sitting. It had moved away from the back door, around a corner, under an archway and up to the table. I was frightened and jumped up and ran upstairs with the dogs at my heels. I jumped into bed and covered my head. I felt very silly and immature doing that but I felt I had to escape from that room—and fast! This presence has made itself felt three times since and always in the same place. My fear is that it will move from room to room following me . . .

'I frequently take my dogs for a run a couple of times during each night and this is why it is difficult for me to fall back to sleep and I enjoy sitting in the kitchen with a cup of tea or something, reading and relaxing with the night in full bloom. I have never felt really frightened or threatened by anything in this house other than what I have explained above. We do live in a very isolated spot and there has been a house on this site since the fourteenth century and the present deeds of the house date back over three hundred years.

'It took me a long time before I had the courage to write to you, basically because I feel silly being the only person to have these strange feelings of foreign bodies. My husband has never heard or felt any of the things that have happened to me and now our friend. When I first heard the conversation of voices in the bedroom my husband said that I was crazy; that is the reason I never told anyone about it. Our friend who has written to you was very unnerved when he disclosed his experiences and only then did my husband accept the facts.'

As I have said I had to say that in view of the fact that most of the reported disturbances had taken place at night-time I did not feel we would be likely to have the opportunity of obtaining a permanent and scientific record of anything during a daylight visit but I asked Mrs Willis to let me know at once if there should be any recurrence of any kind of disturbance. To date I have heard nothing but I still may call one day and I would naturally be very interested to hear from any reader who has knowledge of any similar happenings anywhere.

In the same area my friends Barbara and Duncan McKenzie, who raise the most delightful Cavalier and Irish Water Spaniels, stay with friends two or three times a year in an old thatched cottage where David, the husband in his late thirties, is a little concerned about the ghost child who sits on the landing playing with small lumps of wood.

The wife Sheila saw many times the form of a man on the stairs. He wore a cloak and a big hat, was most often seen during daylight, and she was not in the least concerned. In fact she said how friendly he always seemed and how he appeared to move aside so that she could easily get by, taking off his hat and bowing as he did so.

'Sadly', says Barbara, 'I had never seen either ghost and neither had Duncan or Alison, our eldest daughter, who stays there as often as we do but never, until 1984, at the same time.' David and Sheila have a teenage daughter who often became very distressed when she occupied the bedroom that Barbara and Duncan usually occupied, although to them the house is one of the friendliest they have ever known, with an exceptionally calm and peaceful atmosphere.

Then, staying in the cottage in the middle of a mild autumn, they went to bed very late one night and Barbara, who suffers with a bad hip, didn't get to sleep quickly. She had been in bed about an hour when suddenly it became icy cold and remained so for several hours . . . she tells me she has never felt so cold in her life. She is absolutely certain that she didn't go to sleep all this time although the coldness seemed to anaesthetise the pain in her hip and she snuggled down, hoping to get to sleep. Then she heard a sob and reaching for her spectacles, she put them on and looked round and saw a curly-haired child—it could have been either a girl or a boy but she thinks it was a boy—in a long white nightshirt, with tears streaming down his face which was half in profile as he looked towards her.

No further sound came from the figure and he made no movement, only the tears continued to stream down his cheeks. But then the coldness seemed to lift, very slowly and from the floor upwards—'a most peculiar sensation'! Almost in unison with the gradual warming of the room, the child slowly, very slowly, faded, still without any sound. When the figure had completely disappeared Barbara looked at the clock and found that it was five o'clock in the morning.

A few months later Sheila, who had been ill for a long time, died and Barbara and Duncan went down straightaway to be with David and his daughter and, as Barbara went into the house, she saw a curly-haired 'child' sitting in Sheila's chair, 'smiling tranquilly' at her. She stared at the chair and David said: 'Yes, I keep looking at that chair, expecting to see Sheila sitting there as usual . . .' Barbara looked at him and then back to the chair—which was empty.

Fire Festivals

Among the many ancient fire customs in Britain one of the most famous is the Bridgwater Guy Fawkes Carnival which the local authorities confidently assert dates back, unbroken except for the war years, to the original occasion in 1605 when Guy Fawkes was discovered trying to blow up the Houses of Parliament. The culprit, who so nearly succeeded, persisted through extensive torture at the Tower of London, where his screams are still said to be heard on occasions, that his name was Johnson, but just before he was put to death he signed his confession 'Guido Fawkes'.

It was Parliament who ordered that the fifth of November should be observed as a reminder of the event and as soon as news of the failure of the Gunpowder Plot reached the loyal citizens of Bridgwater, bonfires were lit and torchlight processions were held as they were elsewhere throughout the country; an annual ceremony that to a considerable extent is still observed to this day. In Somerset alone similar Guy Fawkes carnivals are held at Wells, Glastonbury, Highbridge and Spaxton.

Interestingly enough the focus of these events, the effigy of Guy Fawkes, lifesize, clothed, booted, gloved and often carrying a lantern and three matches, has been replaced by other hated personalities. During the First World War the Kaiser often took the place of Guy Fawkes on the bonfire and during the Second World War there was sometimes the unmistakable figure of Hitler. In recent years the Bridgwater Carnival has become largely electrified, for safety reasons, and takes the form of a hundred or more floats powered and lit by electricity. Only during the final few minutes of the Carnival is there any naked flame these days but the tradition lives on.

Fire festivals of much earlier origin include the New Year's Eve custom of 'swinging the fireballs' at Stonehaven, near Aberdeen. Young men make their way through the town carrying balls of wire-netting filled with petrol-soaked rags which they swing in flaming arcs around their heads; a custom that seems to have its origin in Druid fire rituals. In Aberdeen itself the witches used to gather on Beltane Eve and fire was very much a part of their ancient rituals. In the Shetland Isles old pagan customs are even more explicit: at Lerwick for example a burning Norse galley symbolically goes to Valhalla—an exact replica of the send-off given to dead Viking chiefs.

Fire, one of the four elements, has always had magical attributes and it was once the practice to carry fire around a woman after childbirth to preserve both mother and infant from the power of evil spirits who were ready at such times to do mischief and sometimes even carry away the child.

Hatherleigh in Devon has a carnival that has its roots in an ancient fire festival. There is a hunt, a fair in the centre of the village, a children's fancy-dress parade and a great carnival of decorated floats, but the real business of the carnival takes place, to the long-standing disapproval of the police, the night before. Two sledges, each carrying three open-ended barrels on their sides, two on the bottom and one on top, thickly coated with tar and partially filled with inflammable materials, are noisily paraded into position at the top of the village. In the early hours of the morning of the festival one of the sledges of barrels is set alight and some twenty young men haul the sledge down the hill as the flames increase. They run through the streets and into the market carpark where they deposit the remains of their burning load onto a waiting bonfire. At 8.30 in the evening of the carnival the process is repeated with the second sledge. A large torch in the shape of a cross and many smaller flaming torches serve to remind the informed onlooker that this too is a fire festival with pagan origins.

Knowlton, Dorset

Once a thriving village and the capital of a Saxon hundred, today Knowlton is a hamlet but a hamlet with a strange pagan earth circle, built 4000 years ago and believed to have been the scene of human sacrifice; probably an attempt to placate the unquiet atmosphere. Within the ring are the remains of a twelfth-century church built on this pagan site to stop godless rituals, rites and ceremonies that would have been anathema to the Christian Church. This idea of sanctifying, exorcising or counteracting the power of pagan beliefs is to be found in a number of places apart from Knowlton; near the stone circles of Stanton Drew in Avon, for example, at Bryn-celli-ddu, the dark grave-hill of Anglesey, and as we have seen, in the vicinity of the notoriously priapic Cerne Abbas Giant.

LEFT: *Fire Festival scene in Devon.*

At Knowlton the Early Bronze Age henge monument is a haunted place. Not perhaps in the sense that ghosts are seen but rather in the oppressive and peculiar atmosphere of the place. It is an aspect of Knowlton that many people have remarked upon, not least Jacquetta Hawkes, the distinguished archaeologist and widow of J.B. Priestley. She wrote, after visiting Knowlton: 'There is something peculiar in the air of the place, an influence which, as it certainly was not altogether agreeable, might be called a taint', and in her reference to Knowlton in her *Guide to the Prehistoric and Roman Monuments of England and Wales* (1951) she wrote: '. . . perhaps places where men have felt intensely and acted violently never quite rid themselves of the effects; perhaps such feelings are created only in the minds of later beholders—yet even so their survival is real.'

Of all the sites visited by Jacquetta Hawkes, including many ceremonial sites and graves, only Knowlton Circles imparted to her the feeling of a brooding malevolence. John Masefield felt the atmosphere and himself told me he would never forget his visits to Knowlton and he later wrote of the place:

. . . Something passes me and cries as it passes
On the chalk downland bare.

Frank Thorne of Bournemouth has written recently of his experiences at Knowlton Circles; of unreasonable fears and an 'uncontrollable urge to leave' the place. He wrote: 'I went there one November evening close to sunset. I had stopped to see what the responsible government ministry had done to preserve the place, but no sooner was I going through the gate than I knew I must leave; that I was just unwelcome, so I left; quickly and in the wrong direction! I would not cheerfully return there, especially at night.'

A local farmworker, a practical and level-headed individual, detests the place—although he cannot say exactly why; his wife is more direct. She says it is a godless place, and that is strange for there is still the ruined church there.

Once extending to nearly two hundred acres, modern farming machinery has obliterated nearly all but the bank and ditch that hold the old ruined church which has protected the earthwork from

RIGHT: *Knowlton, Dorset: remains of a church built on a pagan site to stop godless rituals.*

Leigh Woods, Bristol, have long had an eerie reputation.

complete obliteration. Now it is no longer an impressive monument but the ancient curse may still be effective. This curse held that anyone damaging the circles brought ill fortune to his family—not to himself but to his family.

A retired accountant visited Knowlton Circles and pocketed a stone from the place as a keepsake. He drove the twenty miles or so home and then, for reasons he still does not fully understand, turned the car round and drove all the way back to replace the stone; and he does not visit Knowlton any more.

Another man, again according to Frank Thorne, went there one night with his girlfriend but they soon left the place when some 'unreasonable fear came upon him and his companion accompanied by an uncontrollable urge to leave the place'. Now he will not visit Knowlton Circles by day, let alone by night!

Thieves are said to have stolen the bell from the church at Knowlton and dumped it in the River Stour when they were pursued. The bell had long been credited with supernatural powers and it is that power that is said to prevent its recovery:

Knowlton bell is stole
And thrown into White Mill Hole
And all the devils in hell
Could never pull up Knowlton bell.

Resting on the river bed between Shapwick and Sturminster Marshall does not prevent it still being heard ringing on occasions in the old ruined church . . .

Sometimes, on sunny summer days, when there are many visitors and children running hither and thither happily, these age-old ceremonial Circles can seem benign but at other times and especially around sunset the air at Knowlton is not quite wholesome; and it becomes a very mysterious place.

Leigh Woods, Bristol, Avon

These woods have long had an eerie reputation and many are the reports of screams and strange happenings in the area which seems to attract the odd and the unusual.

In 1987 when the police were looking for Shirley Banks, a bride of one month, missing for more than three weeks, they discovered, after a nationwide hunt, her car in the 'elegant Leigh Woods area of Bristol, near the city's famous suspension bridge'. A few days later there were reports that the police were linking the disappearance of Shirley Banks with that of estate agent Suzy Lamplugh sixteen months earlier and that they had become aware of the unusual combination of letters and numbers found when the car was discovered. The false number plate was SLP 386S and they wondered whether the SLP was an abbreviation of the name 'Suzy Lamplugh'. Evidence had suggested that the abductor of Suzy Lamplugh had a fascination for letters and it was even felt that the false name given, 'Mr Kipper' could be a deliberate abbreviation of the word 'kidnapper'.

The Leigh Woods area is full of ancient associations and seems to be a very haunted place. Vagrants never sleep in Leigh Woods if they can help it; 'there are strange things in the woods; screams and suchlike . . .' they say. There was an early British camp here before the Romans came; there was an Iron Age promontory fort too and something of these early inhabitants may still linger, in some way which we do not entirely understand, in the numerous reports of odd noises and terrifying happenings that have been reported over the years. Leigh Woods have long had this reputation, especially on dark winter nights when blood-curdling screams and other weird sounds have been heard; sounds for which no natural explanation has ever been discovered. And then there is the behaviour of some dogs in the vicinity. Most dogs behave quite normally in Leigh Woods but sometimes otherwise well-behaved dogs suddenly and inexplicably show all the signs of extreme terror. One dog, a rather fierce Alsatian, always behaves oddly when being exercised in one particular part of the woods. He will jump up on a rock, sit down, lift his head and howl repeatedly. Perhaps this dog and others see or sense some ancient ghostly manifestation that revisits this strangely unquiet spot or perhaps they see the well-known ghost that haunts this place.

The famous suspension bridge was the work of Isambard Kingdom Brunel (1806-59) but he died five years before the bridge he designed was opened and it seems that his unquiet spirit walks in the shadow of his greatest achievement. I have in my possession a score of reported sightings of the ghost of the great man who died relatively young, largely it is said through overwork and the excessive smoking of big cigars. The ghost, a slightly stooping, hurrying figure in double waistcoat, high-collared cut-away overcoat, breeches, a high and straight top hat and the inevitable cigar, is usually seen for a moment or distinctly glimpsed for a few seconds, before it passes behind or disappears into some natural obstruction and is seen no more—until the next time. What is interesting is that the figure has been seen by a wide variety of people, on different occasions, who have had no previous knowledge that the ghost of Brunel walks in the Leigh Woods area.

LEFT: *Sometimes dogs undergo a character change in these woods.*

Brunel, second from the right, awaiting the launch of the Great Eastern, *the wonder of the seas. His ghost, complete with the inevitable cigar, has been seen hereabouts.*

Interestingly enough Brunel designed the *Great Eastern*, the 'wonder of the seas' and the mother of ocean liners, and the *Great Eastern* was a haunted ship. Dozens of workmen were killed or injured during the construction and launching of the ship and always, from time to time, the unexplained sound of 'constant hammering from below' was repeatedly heard. Captain Harrison complained to his chief engineer (as others had before him) and he investigated again and again but could not account for the deafening noises that always seemed to be heard before a misfortune occurred aboard ship. Eventually, during the break-up of the ship that had become 'the white elephant of the seas', the wall of a compartment in the inner shell on the port side was broken down and inside demolition workers found a carpet bag of rusted tools and a human skeleton. They were thought to be the remains of a workman who had accidentally become entombed between the hulls during some stage of the construction of the ship and whose ghost, for thirty years, haunted the ship to warn others of approaching misfortune.

The Merry Maidens, St Buryan, Cornwall

Many of Britain's scores of stone circles, ranging from a dozen feet in diameter to hundreds of feet across, are to be found in Cornwall and of these one of the most famous is known as the Merry Maidens in West Penwith. Some, perhaps most, of the rarely-visited and less accessible circles appear to emanate powerful, almost tangible, currents of energy.

William Crossing, in his *Crossing's Guide to Dartmoor* (1912) points out that various suggestions have been made for these stone circles: 'that they were intended for gymnastic performances; that they were part of serpent temples; that they formed the processional roads of the Druids; that they were race courses; that they were once roofed and formed shelters; that they represented armies drawn up in battle array; that they were intended to guide people over the moors in misty weather; that they have an astronomical significance; and that they are a representation of passages that led to the chamber in a tumulus . . .' To these varied suggestions might be added the idea that the mysterious stone circles are circles of power and that they have some connection with visitors from other planets. On the face of it, it does seem strange that so many of these circles exist, yet we have no definite idea as to their origin or purpose.

My namesake Guy Underwood—as far as I know no relation—carried out an investigation of 'sacred sites' by means of the divining rod. In his monumental *Patterns of the Past* (published posthumously in 1969), he suggested that many if not all of these stone circles and other ancient sites were situated over blind water springs which produced an 'earth or geodetic force' which the

philosophers and priests of the old religions seem to have been aware of and to have been involved with: the generative force of nature. What is undeniable is that many people have found that a 'force' or 'power' emanates from some if not all of these mysterious stone circles. Colin Wilson has no doubt that this is so; T.C. Lethbridge was convinced the circles were 'charged' with energy which visitors from outer space could have homed in on, a kind of 'landing light'; and my own postbag on the subject leaves no doubt that the stone circles of the ancients can exert a force on present-day visitors.

Colin Wilson's experience was a particularly interesting one. He had only tried dowsing, or divining, once before, in his own garden, without any result, although his wife Joy obtained a strong reaction. At the Merry Maidens Colin used a pendulum and found that it twitched violently as he approached the stones, although he felt nothing, and as he moved beyond the limit of the stone circle, which is supposed to be surrounded by a line of power, he obtained the most powerful and violent reactions; when he reached the centre of the circle he again found a powerful reaction.

The Merry Maidens—the name conjures up a picture of impious girls dancing and laughingly ignoring the dark scowls of their elders—have been built on a slight slope and now consist of nineteen stones of local granite. Some if not all of the stones appear to have been 'dressed' to shape before being placed in position; certainly the tops of all the stones have been carefully levelled. There is a gap at the east end of the circle and this could have been the original entrance and, as with other stone circles, there is a taller, larger stone at the west end, possibly acting as an astronomical marker or indicating the May Day sunrise. Some outlying stones may have been territorial markers or even 'ancestor' stones, as Aubrey Bone points out in *Rings of Stone* (Frances Lincoln, 1979); at all events the real significance of these stone circles is now lost to us.

The Merry Maidens leave different impressions on different people. To me they are the silent witnesses of a past way of life with a meaning that we have yet to discover and they contain a power of some kind that is almost pulsating in its intensity; they are truly

LEFT: *'T.C. Lethbridge was convinced that circles were "charged" with energy . . .'*

fascinating. Tom Lethbridge found them equally fascinating and while dowsing over the stones in an attempt to date them, he experienced mild electric shocks, almost as though the stones were some kind of battery. So powerful was the reaction that the pendulum in Lethbridge's hand described a circle that was almost horizontal to the ground. He concluded, this scientist, explorer and archaeologist, that some great force was stored in the stones. He persisted with his pendulum and gave his opinion as to the age of the Merry Maidens stone circle. Later, by more sophisticated methods, including Carbon 14 dating, Lethbridge's findings were confirmed.

Tom Lethbridge believed the stones that form the Merry Maidens are imbued with a form of bio-energy and that this stored energy, possibly induced by frenzied religious dances and ceremonies that certainly took place about these stones, was familiar to and used by spacemen visiting our planet. Certainly the belief is that maidens dancing here on the sacred days were turned to stone. Some say the stones still dance on certain days of the year. Yet cattle seem unaffected by any 'power' in the stones and graze peacefully enough. Whatever the truth about the Merry Maidens the simple sight of them exerts a mysterious influence over visitors to this day.

Minions, Cornwall

A group of stones here on Craddock Moor is known as The Hurlers and are said by some to have once been men who played, on a sacred day, the old Cornish sport known as hurling and were turned to stone for their sins. These three stone circles on Bodmin Moor share this legend, or something very similar, with solitary or groups of standing or leaning stones, the Blind Fiddler, north-west of Catchall, the Pipers and the Merry Maidens near Boleigh. Divine judgement for Sabbath-breaking, the profaning of the Lord's Day, dates

LEFT: *The famous Merry Maidens in Penwith, drawn by Felicity Young in the autumn of 1987.*

from the seventeenth-century or possibly earlier, a period when the idea of divine retribution was very popular and indeed it continued well into the eighteenth century and even later. Vehement pulpit oratory played a major part in producing such legends.

Incidentally the term 'Maiden' as applied to stone circles seems to be limited to five sites in Cornwall and one in Devon; it may well be therefore that the term is derived from the Cornish *maen* meaning a stone; the change from *maen* to maiden probably taking place as the Cornish language became obsolete.

St Columb Major, also in Cornwall, was traditionally a centre for hurling which was a game played with a wooden ball covered with silver gilt; a game that is supposed to have had very ancient origins. It was played by two teams, often two parishes, with forty or sixty men on each side. The object was to get the ball and carry it off to one's own goal, sometimes three or four miles distant, while players from the opposing team attempted to intercept you. Strangely enough it was usually played on a Sunday afternoon. Passing the ball from hand to hand brought good luck to those who touched it and this folk memory could well be a vestigial reminder of sun worship.

The Hurlers share with other stone circles the belief that the stones cannot be counted correctly, a belief that is to be found in print as early as 1602 in the case of the Hurlers. Only in the case of Stonehenge (1586) does an earlier published or written account refer to this belief. All the others, Stanton Drew, Avon (1749), the Rollright Stones, Oxfordshire (1853), Long Meg and her Daughters, Cumbria (1690), Swinside, Cumbria (1939), Y Naw Carreg, Carmarthenshire (1917) and Callanish, Lewis and Harris (1880), have various stories of people who have counted them and in some cases (Stonehenge and Stanton Drew) suffered dire misfortune or even death for counting the stones correctly. In the case of the Hurlers there is a story of a baker placing loaves of bread on each of the stones in 1675 and counting them by the number of loaves left. Even today one can find various numbers chalked on some of the groups of standing stones showing where visitors have attempted to count the stones. The earliest reference to the Hurlers comes from R. Carew's *Survey of Cornwall* (1602) where he says: 'A redoubled numbering never eveneth with the first . . . but far stranger is the country people's report that once they were men, and for their hurling upon the Sabbath, so metamorphosed.'

The Hurlers photographed by Ray Bishop in 1987.

The Hurlers were, in all probability, erected in the Bronze Age 'for purposes unknown' says Jennifer Westwood in her authoritative *Albion: A Guide to Legendary Britain* (1985). Be that as it may there is persistent evidence from different people that some stone circles and the Hurlers in particular are 'charged up' in some way and can give people who lean against them a distinct 'shock'. It could well be that the old dances and frenzied celebrations at these stone circles had the effect and purpose of charging them in much the same way that a dynamo is activated.

New Forest, Hampshire

In July 1983 Dr John Beloff, at that time President of the Society for Psychical Research, wrote to me from the Department of Psychology, University of Edinburgh, enclosing the translation of an article from a Dutch magazine concerning a very strange occurrence. It had been sent to Dr Beloff by Leif Aarstad, a member of the Danish Society for Psychical Research. The gist of the lengthy and illustrated article is as follows.

One day in August 1979 seventeen-year-old Lois Suzanne Elledge was walking in the New Forest during the course of a visit to her aunt, Margaret Elledge, when she saw ahead of her a woman with a little girl. There was nothing particularly remarkable about the couple although Lois did think they appeared to be dressed in rather an old-fashioned manner.

'They made no particular impression on me,' Lois said afterwards. 'But I saw them quite distinctly, and then suddenly they disappeared. When I saw them, they were no more than some twenty steps ahead of me, but then, as we came to a clearing, they had suddenly gone.'

Puzzled, Lois entered the clearing and looked about her and among the trees but the woman and child were nowhere to be seen and there appeared to be no place they could have hidden themselves. 'I could not understand where they had gone; but then I stopped thinking about it and went on. On my way back I could not help thinking of it again as I walked into the clearing and I looked around me but there was no sign of the woman or the child.'

When she returned to her aunt, Lois related her strange experience and her aunt suggested that Lois had been subjected to an optical illusion and there had been no-one in the forest but Lois maintained obstinately that she had seen two persons in the forest and next day she returned to the forest to see whether she could see anything of the couple again. For three hours she sat on the stump

LEFT: *An artist's impression of the ghostly pair in the New Forest: a sighting which led to an incredible discovery.*

Two faces of the New Forest in autumn.

of a tree but she saw nobody and at last she returned home. There she found a message from her aunt awaiting her. 'I have gone to Lyndhurst to speak to Kenneth Smith; he is a local historian, and I shall ask him whether he knows anything about the two persons you have seen.'

'Only then,' Lois said later, 'did I begin to ponder over what I had seen. I do not believe in ghosts and spirits of the dead or, rather, I did not believe in things of that sort until I read my aunt's message. Why should she seek a local historian, unless she suspected that I *had* seen something, something which Kenneth Smith might know about? I decided to return to the clearing in the forest each day to see whether the woman and child would turn up again. Next day, immediately after breakfast, I set out for the forest and I took with me a packed lunch and a thermos with coffee and I sat down on the trunk of the tree and waited, as I had done the previous day.

At 10.35 that morning Lois again saw the woman and the child. They came into the clearing and again they were holding each other's hands just as they had been the first time she saw them; and

they took no heed of her and crossed the clearing. 'Hallo, good morning!' called Lois, but neither the woman nor the child reacted to her call. They walked straight on, as if Lois did not exist. They reached some low bushes about five yards from Lois and there they suddenly vanished into thin air! For a moment Lois felt very frightened and she could hardly believe her own eyes. She pulled herself together and hurried home as fast as she could and told her aunt about what she had seen. Shortly afterwards Kenneth Smith and another man, whom he introduced as Sergeant John Blake, called to see her.

After Lois had told the two men everything she had seen, the sergeant brought out some photographs and handed them to Lois asking her to be kind enough to examine them and tell him whether she recognised any of the people in the photographs. 'Take your time,' he added. 'We want you to be absolutely sure.'

Lois studied the photographs carefully one by one and then suddenly she stopped at a hand-coloured photograph of a woman aged about thirty-four and a little girl who seemed to be between ten and eleven years of age. 'That is the woman I saw,' Lois said without hesitation, 'and it is also the same child. I am absolutely certain; I have seen them twice and the second time I watched them very carefully. What is all this about, anyway?'

The sergeant looked hesitatingly at Lois's aunt, before he replied: 'In 1941 a woman and a child disappeared from their home in Southampton, not far from here. I am unable to say anything more now but I shall be very grateful if you will show us the exact place where you saw them disappear . . .'

Next morning at nine o'clock, accompanied by several policemen, Lois and her aunt all went to the forest to the clearing where Lois had twice seen the woman and child disappear. After she had indicated the exact spot, from several angles, she and her aunt were sent home and the policemen began digging. About noon the sergeant returned to Lois and her aunt.

'We have found them,' he said. 'Exactly where you told us they vanished, we found the skeletons of a woman and a child. We have not yet identified them but certain objects were found and also their teeth and we are virtually sure that we have found the remains of Sandra Sinclair and her daughter Marie, who disappeared in August, 1941.'

Lois returned to her home in London but three weeks later a member of the London Society for Psychical Research called to see her and questioned her about what she had seen in the New Forest and a week later a police officer arrived and asked her to assist them in their enquiries by travelling to Southampton where an inquest was to be carried out on the remains of the woman and child; they wanted to confirm what she had seen, for without her the two skeletons would never have been found.

In Southampton Lois was told that the dead bodies had finally been identified as Sandra Sinclair and her daughter Marie. It appeared from evidence given that Sandra Sinclair had been married to a soldier serving in North Africa and while he was away she had had an affair with a thirty-seven-year-old man named Ethan Loring Anderson, who had been discharged from military service on medical grounds. The police found and interrogated Anderson who denied having anything to do with the disappearances and the police had to dismiss the case on account of lack of evidence, although they suspected him of having murdered the woman and the child and disposing of their corpses in the forest.

Experts then confirmed that the woman had been strangled and that her skull had been smashed with a blunt instrument, possibly a hammer. They also assumed that the child had been strangled but this could not be definitely established. In all the circumstances it was assumed that Sandra Sinclair and her daughter had been murdered by some person or persons unknown and the police were continuing with their investigations.

Ethan Loring Anderson was then traced to a boarding house in Portsmouth and he was taken to a police station and subjected to a long interrogation but the old man denied any knowledge of the murders and maintained that he had last seen the woman and her daughter about a week before they disappeared. Again the police released Anderson on account of lack of evidence and even today they have no concrete knowledge of the person or persons who murdered the woman and her daughter, or why, but they do have a theory.

'We believe,' a detective constable has revealed, 'that Sandra had a lover, that she discontinued the relationship, and that he murdered her. Afterwards he had to murder the child because she had seen what he had done. Most likely under cover of darkness he transported the corpses to a remote spot in the New Forest and there he buried them, believing they would never be found.'

On 29 January 1980, says the Danish article, Ethan Loring Anderson disappeared from the boarding house where he was living and two days later he was found, drowned in the sea outside Portsmouth. The inquest came to the conclusion that he had committed suicide but he had left no farewell letter so it will probably never be established whether it was he who committed the terrible double-murder that led to two ghosts who revealed where their bodies lay . . .

Newlyn East, Cornwall

The fifteenth-century church here is celebrated far and wide on account of the flourishing fig tree springing from the south wall. Tradition has it that anyone who plucks a leaf from the tree will die within a year and many are the tales of people who have succumbed to the curse in this mysterious place.

The legend that the tree brings disaster to anyone who tampers with it is a very old one. The tree itself is at least one hundred years old; it indisputably grows out of the wall of the church, which possesses a beautiful Norman font and some handsome carvings, and it seems likely that the roots of the tree go down to an ancient well used by monks many centuries ago. A verse detailing the unusual properties of the tree is affixed to the church wall.

Understandably perhaps the rector has difficulty in finding a local handyman to keep the giant tree tidy and some years ago the Reverend Peter Denny told me that he felt under an obligation to inform applicants about the curse. He told me, 'At least six persons who have at some time or other cut back the fig tree have met with tragedy. The last man who pruned it died in a tractor accident; and there is a story of an Australian who picked one of the leaves and died on the voyage home.'

The strange fig tree springing from the south wall of the church at Newlyn East.

The former Poet Laureate, Sir John Betjeman, who told the author of 'the most terrifying cliff scenery in all Cornwall'.

The more common story associated with trees that grow out of church walls or through tombs is that they represent an answer to a disbeliever who has challenged whatever powers there be to provide evidence by growing in this way.

Padstow, Cornwall

Pepper Hole, near Padstow, which John Betjeman once told me he found 'the most terrifying cliff scenery in all Cornwall' is well worth

a visit. It is a truly mysterious place. Suddenly in the springy turf one comes across a hole about fifty yards in diameter, where black slate veined with white and green falls sheer for two hundred feet, and at the bottom the sunlit Atlantic foams under an arch over unapproachable boulders. On the way to Pepper Hole from Padstow, a truly glorious walk, the Camel Estuary widens from little more than a quarter of a mile where the ferry crosses to Rock, to a full mile at Stepper Point with its 227-feet-high tower or 'day-mark' for shipping. About halfway along the walk one looks down on the Doom Bar, a brown discolouration that stretches very nearly right across the wide entrance to the estuary. The name is an apt one, for a ship that misses the narrow channel on the west side, so narrow that her yardarms almost scrape the rocks, is doomed beyond all hope of saving. The main channel has now moved over to the eastern side, but this western channel, no longer navigable, still provides a sheltered anchorage at the seaward end. Those who have seen a heavy squall strike the mouth of the harbour, whipping the water into foam from side to side, will understand the significance of the name. According to legend the Doom Bar is the work of a mermaid, the protectress of Padstow. When she was mortally wounded by an arrow released by a young man, she threw a handful of sand towards the town with a curse, and so the bar was formed—a bar that presents to this day a real hazard to shipping.

While in the vicinity a visit should be made to Tregudda Gorge, a grand sight at any time and magnificent when the sea is rough. South again is Porthmissen Bridge, a natural arch, and nearby there is the curious Round Hole which is in fact a blow hole.

A little further south, at Harlyn Bay, there used to be a museum containing a number of antiquities excavated on the site; in all probability an Iron Age cemetery. In 1900 workmen sinking foundations for a house uncovered several caskets containing human bones. One of the richest discoveries of prehistoric remains ever made in the British Isles, they proved to be Celtic burials which probably took place 2500 years ago. Altogether more than two hundred caskets were found, all the skeletons being in the crouched position, all laying on their left side and all had their heads to the north. The

LEFT: *Doom Bar in the Camel Estuary seen from the air.*

remains were found under ten to fifteen feet of sand which may have preserved them over the ensuing twenty-five centuries. A few years ago, due to development, the museum was closed and the main exhibits moved to the County Museum at Truro.

I remember, in the 1950s, visiting the little museum and viewing some of the remains in the ground, covered by sheet glass. The curator, at that time, told me that he had often felt a curious atmosphere in the vicinity of these ancient bones and that on several occasions he thought he had glimpsed vague moving forms which he was totally unable to explain. He also said that there was no doubt that the bones were sometimes moved although they were in fact completely sealed and inaccessible.

'The main road from Padstow along the coast,' says Baring-Gould in his *Book of Folklore* (1913) 'cuts through this ancient cemetery and it is interesting to note that this portion of the road has ever been dreaded by passengers at night as haunted.'

Polperro, Cornwall

Certainly one of the most picturesque of all Cornwall's villages but perhaps not widely acknowledged as a 'mysterious' place, Polperro, where the houses seem to tumble onto each other down the steep and rocky valley, is in fact full of legend, superstition, strange beliefs and even stranger happenings—not in the distant past but today.

Almost every old house here has a secret entrance, a secret cupboard or a secret exit, all leftovers from the days when smuggling was a profitable and comparatively safe business. At low tide the place always seems to be full of screaming gulls and no Cornishman will ever ill-treat one; exactly as it must have been for hundreds of years. Today, all day and every day, it is difficult to find a chimney-pot or a roof that does not carry a huge gull; each perhaps the re-embodiment of a drowned sailor.

LEFT: *Tregudda Gorge: '. . . a grand sight at any time.'*

On the western side of the harbour entrance the great Peak Rock juts out from the base of the Chapel Hill and under Chapel Hill is a cavern, known as Willy Willcock's Hole which is said to extend into the bowels of the hill more than a quarter of a mile away. Be that as it may, the generally accepted story suggests that many years ago a local man, Will Willcocks, decided to see whether he could establish the truth and he crept, with some difficulty, through the narrow opening at the back of the cave but must have soon become stuck firm or lost his way in the maze of tunnels that may lie under the hill; at all events he was never seen again. However, his shrieks of despair—or those of his ghost—are still said to be heard in the vicinity on occasions, usually after nightfall.

Those who seek for tangible signs of the Devil himself in Cornwall should look well at the fissure in the rock near Chapel Pool and at the deep impression in that hoof-shaped pool. Legend has it that the Devil, ascending from the realms of darkness, chose to emerge at a spot near the harbour entrance at Polperro and as he rose from

Gulls feature strongly in our folklore.

Polperro, a most picturesque Cornish village where houses seem to tumble on to each other.

below in his fiery chariot, driven by a gigantic and jet-black steed, the rocks gave way before him and the rent near Chapel Pool remains to this day to confound disbelievers. The Devil's horse, evidently delighted at the refreshing air of the upper world, reared in wild triumph and planted one hoof upon the ground, leaving a strange and deep impression in Chapel Pool.

Polperro is in fact mysterious in several ways. At the top of Landividdy Hill there are the fragmentary remains of All Saints Well, almost hidden in a hedge. The edifice that once surrounded a perennial spring may have practically disappeared but the fame of the well lives on. Its special virtues were the curative powers it possessed for eye complaints and, even today, if the due ceremonies and rites are performed on three successive mornings, before sunrise, beneficial results are said to be guaranteed.

Nearby Talland Bay, where a path descends from the cliffs to sea level, is the site of one of the oldest stories of Cornish Piskies. As

'Polperro is in fact mysterious in several ways.'

recounted by Maurice Bizley some years back, it concerned a boy, returning one evening from Polperro, many years ago, to his home just inland from Talland, a small hamlet known as Porthallow, when he was surprised to suddenly hear a voice say, 'I'm for Porthallow Green'. Hoping for company the boy repeated the sentence himself, 'I'm for Porthallow Green' and immediately found himself on the Green, surrounded by a crowd of dancing Piskies.

Almost at once another tiny voice said, 'I'm for Seaton Beach' and the adventurous boy repeated, 'I'm for Seaton Beach' and in an instant he found himself on that fine expanse of sand between Looe and Plymouth. Soon one of his new-found Piskie friends shouted, 'I'm for the King of France's cellar' and when the boy repeated this, he immediately found himself in a spacious cellar engaged with his tiny companions in tasting the rich wines. Having had their fill they passed through the cellar, up the stairs and into some grand rooms fitted out with great splendour. One room had tables laid with fine plate and rich foods and beautiful drinking vessels. The boy, wishing to take home some memento of his wonderful travels, slipped a silver goblet into his pocket.

A little while later one of the Piskies cried 'I'm for Seaton Beach' and repeating the cry himself the boy found himself back again on those sands, with the state of the tide hardly altered, so quick had been his journey! When he cried out 'I'm for Porthallow Green' he swiftly found himself at his final destination and there the Piskies left him and the boy returned to his home, much excited and full of his adventures. When he told his story his mother said, 'The boy's mazed!' but to prove his story the boy produced the silver goblet and it is said that the goblet remained in the family for many generations but now, alas, it is no longer available to show to those who may doubt the story.

In Polperro, as at Padstow, Marazion and St Ives in Cornwall alone, some roof tiles are said to have a life of their own and to 'wake up and roam about at midnight'. Polperro was supposed to be the one place in Cornwall, perhaps in the whole of Christendom, where if you rose very early on Easter Day, you might 'see the sun dance'; while on the first day of May, if you were seen not sporting a 'lucky' May blossom in your buttonhole, you were likely to be seized and dipped or sprinkled with water.

Royal Fort House, Bristol, Avon

Both the site and the existing Georgian Royal Fort House at Bristol, now housing the University of Bristol departments of music and theology, have a fascinating history and a curious reputation.

A house here belonged to the family of Tyndall for five centuries; in the sixteenth century William Tyndall translated the Bible into English and in so doing caused a considerable storm and social upheaval.

Upheaval of another kind took place when the Great Fort, built at the time of the Civil War as part of the fortifications for Bristol, surrendered to Cromwell's forces under Sir Thomas Fairfax. Prince Rupert, its Governor, appointed by King Charles, found himself dismissed from all his offices and lived to see the old Royal Fort House totally destroyed apart from the pentagonal structure approached from St Michael's Hill. In 1638 'Tyndall's' was used for the isolation of plague victims. Later it was a school for girls and then, through the wealth acquired in the slave trade—the house in Marguerite Steen's novel *The Sun is my Undoing* is in fact Royal Fort House—the Tyndall family built the present edifice to the design of James Bridges, whose other works include Bristol Bridge. Under the present hall the original vaulted cellars are still used, for storage.

Ghost enthusiast Margaret Royal told me in 1980 that there were reports of ghostly manifestations at Royal Fort House from practically all its turbulent, unsavoury and pleasant periods of history.

There is for instance the sombre figure of Prince Rupert himself, son of the 'winter king' of Bohemia, Frederick V and of Elizabeth, daughter of James I of England, who wanders about the gatehouse area, seemingly pondering on the fact that he surrendered Bristol without fighting to the uttermost and then rode to Oxford with his enemies . . . there is, too, a prosperous-looking gentleman in seventeenth-century morning clothes, strutting about the ground floor near the beautiful staircase and at other times standing nearby apparently contemplating the original model for the house . . . then there is the half-glimpsed grotesque forms of figures who may be plaque victims and the sounds of girlish laughter and light running footsteps reportedly heard during the evenings and at weekends when the house is empty of students; a psychic echo perhaps from the days when the girls' school was here . . . and some female figures have been reportedly seen but details are too sketchy for the forms to be accurately dated.

The sound of unexplained footsteps is the commonest manifestation at the Royal Fort House and it has been noticed that these

RIGHT: *Both the site and the existing Georgian Royal Fort House at Bristol, now housing the University of Bristol Departments of Music and Theology, have a curious reputation.*

Royal Fort House gardens.

sounds and other ghostly happenings are reported most frequently on sunny afternoons; at such times a female figure has been seen from the gardens in an upper room, a figure that seemed to be engrossed in some activity but certainly had no normal reality. Some years ago an electrical engineer was carrying out repairs in the upper part of the house when he was suddenly confronted by the form of an old woman who seemed be be friendly but curiously interested in what he was doing. When she suddenly and inexplicably disappeared, the electrician left the room and refused to return.

There have been stories of unsavoury psychic happenings associated with the two wells and also with the underground passage that traverses the lawns in the direction of the River Avon but in the main the daytime ghosts at this historic house walk in a tranquil and friendly atmosphere; but that it is a mysterious place few would deny, few that is among those who have experienced its strange and swiftly changing atmosphere when it is deserted by the living.

Sampford Peverell, Devon

Here a house that was destroyed by fire in the 1940s was the scene of classic poltergeist disturbances in the nineteenth century; a case that received full and firsthand treatment from the Reverend Caleb Colton in his *Narrative of the Sampford Ghost* (published in Tiverton in 1810). The disturbance included thunderous sounds; blows by invisible hands; objects moving of there own volition and a wealth of other apparently inexplicable happenings which continued for more than three years. Many years after the 'poltergeist' infestation it was discovered that the property had a number of double walls which could have had some bearing on the matter. I included details of this curious case in my Bossiney volume on the *Ghosts of Devon*. The Ghost House, as it was called, is no more, the trouble ceased as suddenly and as mysteriously as it began, but not a few residents recall the curious story of another haunted house at Sampford Peverell, a cottage which a Ghost Club member visited in the company of Colonel Cecil Powney, OBE.

Here pictures removed themselves from walls, to lie quietly undamaged on the floor; vases were flung from shelves by unseen hands; tables and chairs were seen to move as if propelled by some unseen force and from time to time the soft tread of footsteps would be heard that was totally inexplicable. Nothing was reported to have been seen, however.

The Ghost Club member, Miss Nell St John Montague, discovered that the then owner's mother, an elderly lady who had recently died, might be responsible for the disturbances although by all accounts she had lived peacefully at the cottage and there seemed to be no reason why she would want to upset her son and his family. Miss St John Montague takes up the story:

'It was a fine afternoon when I motored down from town with my distinguished friend and was met by two other friends who lived in the neighbourhood. We all four rather looked on the affair as an interesting mystery, but none of us took it too seriously. When we reached the pretty, two-storey cottage, a crowd of anxious sight-seers crowded in front of the gate, on which was hung a board with the notice roughly painted, "No admittance".

'Ignoring this we went up the path and in a moment a white-faced woman opened the door and with a pale, haggard man and two terrified-looking children, bade us welcome.

'It was arranged that while my friends went through to a room upstairs I should remain alone in the front parlour. The room I went into was bright and most *un*-haunted-looking; being neatly and colourfully furnished. I drew up an armchair before the fire and settling myself comfortably was thinking that nothing could appear less in keeping with the ghostly accounts I had heard of moving furniture and creeping footsteps when I suddenly started. I was conscious that something was moving behind me and even as I turned my head quickly to see who had entered, a large armchair in the middle of the room began to move slowly and deliberately towards me.

'Closer it came, and closer still, while I sat rigid and aghast; then I heard the distinct sound of laboured breathing and the echo of feet moving as if one dragged heavily behind the other. In one movement and in a split second I reached the door, wrenched it open and called loudly for my friends, telling them I could not remain alone in the room.

'As soon as they joined me I closed the door and told them what I had seen; they stared incredulously . . . and the next moment one of them pointed excitedly: "Look! Oh! Look!" Slowly, as if supported from falling quickly by invisible hands, we all saw a large picture at the end of the room *creep* down the wall and slide gently on to the carpet before us. Each of us heard at the same moment slow foot-steps in the room and we all noticed the sound of a dragging foot. Then right past my face a small miniature hanging on the wall seemed to fly and rolled at our feet.

'For a short time we remained completely still, hardly daring to breathe; then one of my companions suggested I should go upstairs and see the room they had just left. Leaving them in the haunted room I made my way up the tiny staircase into the biggest bedroom. It was a simple room with very little furniture in it. As I stood looking round I heard the echo of heavy feet, one foot evidently being dragged behind the other, and turning sharply I saw an old woman. She was dressed in a short, thick skirt, and wore a shawl over her head, and she dragged one of her feet as if it was paralysed.

'I gathered myself together and addressed the figure in a voice I hardly recognised as my own: "I am sorry if I am in your room," I said, "but I came to see if I could find out anything about the ghost ..." I paused and she lifted her head and faced me. "I can't rest ..." Her voice was low, but very clear. "I can't rest . . ."

'For the moment I imagined she meant that I had disturbed her by coming to the room and was about to apologise. Then I wondered if I was dreaming for the old woman had completely disappeared! It was as if she had faded through the wall; she had gone right before my eyes. I hurriedly returned downstairs to the sitting-room and breathlessly told my friends what I had seen. Then we sent for the owner of the cottage and I asked him: "Who is the old woman I saw upstairs, who walks with a bad limp, and drags one foot after her?"

'The man's face grew more haggard and I seemed to see actual terror in his eyes. "My mother dragged her foot, madam," he replied, adding in a whisper: "She died in that room."

'When we asked him if he knew of any reason why she could not rest he declared he did not, and as time was getting on, we left, as two of us had to return to town before it was too late.

'A week later I received another almost frenzied request to try once more and solve the mystery of the strange happenings in the haunted cottage. Pictures still came down from the walls, I was told, furniture and ornaments still moved about as if on wings. Rather reluctantly I motored down, accompanied by my two daughters and Colonel Cecil Powney.

'Leaving them, after our arrival, in the sitting-room I went upstairs and sitting on the chair beside the window, looked out across the garden. The next instant I turned, as I heard the sound of a moving chair being pushed towards me, and the other echo of the now familiar dragging foot. As I wondered whether I should spring up and make good my escape or wait for developments, I saw, sitting on the now stationary chair, the same old woman I had seen before. My fear, when I had first heard the chair moving, disappeared, and I found I could look at her.

' "Why do you come?" I asked her. "Why do you do all this to terrify your son and grandchildren?"

'Slowly she spoke in reply. "I can't rest. I can't rest. They burned my letter . . . they destroyed my letter." I was possessed of a courage I did not know I possessed and I leaned forward, staring at her. "Do go away . . ." I begged her. "Do go away . . ."

'Her eyes met mine and I was struck by their heaviness and reproach. "They burned my letter," she said again, and her voice was slow and monotonous. "They destroyed it . . ." For a moment there was silence and again I stared into those heavy eyes. "Do go away," I begged her. "Your grandchildren are ill from terror because of what is happening. Do go."

'There was silence once more, and I suddenly felt a strange inclination to scream aloud. Then I saw the old woman move and regain her feet. I saw her raise her claw-like hands in the air as if clutching for support to help her to rise. "I will go . . ." she said. "I will go . . ."

'I heard no more. I saw no more. Only in my ears came the echo of a loud crash . . . then oblivion. When, some time later, they found me, they thought the dead faint I was in was death itself. A strange incident lay in the fact that the bedclothes, long unused, had been neatly turned back, as if in preparation for an occupant of the bed, while those who entered in search of me were struck by a strangely ominous and icy chill. It was some time before I, who had never fainted before, came to, and when I did I realised my one craving was to see the old woman's son.

'Presently he came, reluctantly, accompanied by his wife who was full of scared solicitude for my health. "What letter of your mother's was burned, and keeps her from resting?" I asked. The man shook his head. "I don't know . . . I don't know," he answered hurriedly. His wife uttered a loud moan and throwing her apron over her head, cried: "Your mother has told her," she said, sobbing. "Tell the lady the truth."

'Then I learned the story. Years ago the dead woman had given a sacred promise to one she loved to leave a letter containing the

LEFT: *Sampford Peverell, Devon: ghost of an old woman. 'She was dressed in a short, thick skirt, and wore a shawl over her head, and I noticed she dragged one of her feet . . .'*

solution of a life-long secret, which amounted to the clearing up of a mystery. That vow she had kept faithfully. She *had* written a letter and left it addressed to the one to whom she had made the promise. After her death her son had found the letter addressed to the other person. "By accident," he said quickly, "I threw it on the fire with some other papers . . ." I met his guilt-shadowed eyes, and for an instance the silence was only broken by his deep breathing and the sobs of his wife. "Unless you send for the one to whom that letter was written," I said at last, "and confess your mother kept her vow, your cottage will surely be haunted by her. That one she loved must know that she kept her promise to him."

'Some days later, terrified by further mysterious happenings, the son reluctantly sent for the other person and testified to him that the dead woman had kept her word and was innocent of having broken her vow, although through no fault of hers the mystery of the life-long secret which so tormented him could never now be revealed this side of the grave.

'It was a strange coincidence that at ten minutes to four, the very time I saw the old woman for the second and last time, my watch stopped, the clocks in the cottage stopped, Colonel Powney's watch stopped and my daughter's wrist-watch stopped—all at the same time: ten minutes to four o'clock. Was it to indicate the passing of a spirit back to its own happier sphere?'

St Buryan, near Land's End, Cornwall

The churchyard here has been the subject of so many strange happenings and odd experiences that it must warrant a corner in any collection of mysterious places. There are several interesting epitaphs carved on the gravestones here and one, an example of the widespread distrust of lawyers, bears repetition:

Here lie John and Richard Benn
Two lawyers and two honest men.
God works miracles now and then.

The fifteenth-century church is dedicated to St Buriena, a

daughter of a King of Ireland, and St Buryan itself has many legends and associations with fairies and with witches. A local cow's milk was supposedly only available to fairies and those with fairy sympathies and nearby is the Crowz-an-Wra, an ancient monument whose name means, literally, 'the witch's cross'. Here, too, is to be found the legend of William Noy who was abducted by the little people but he was overjoyed at finding they had also taken away his long lost sweetheart Grace Hutchens whom he had thought dead when she had disappeared three years before. Seeing her in the power of the fairies he recalled that a garment turned inside out would break a fairy spell so he pulled off a glove, turning it inside out, and threw it at the little people. They vanished immediately but alas so did Grace and from that time onward William Noy pined for her and after he was dead and buried in St Buryan's churchyard his ghost kept up the vigil, waiting, looking and seeking for his one and only love. Certainly there are many reports of an unidentified form flitting about the churchyard at nights that may or may not be the ghost of William Noy.

The churchyard was in the news in 1975 when Lady Lucy Russell, whose father succeeded to the earldom when philosopher Bertrand Russell died in 1970, set fire to herself in some sort of ritual while clinging to one of the two 'sun wheel crosses' on a large pyramid-shaped granite monument in the churchyard; where parts of the controversial film *Straw Dogs* was shot.

Matches and scorch marks, together with an empty paraffin can, were found on the top of the pyramid and it seems that the twenty-four-year old Lady Lucy set fire to herself before fleeing from the churchyard, blazing like a human torch, and collapsing in the village smithy. The blacksmith said at the time, 'She was burning from head to foot when she ran into our yard; with two other men I managed to smother the flames with horse blankets but she was so badly burned that we didn't know whether it was a man or a woman.' She died soon afterwards in hospital.

Lady Lucy lived in the nearby coastal village of Porthcurno with its haunted cove and mysterious Logan Rock, once a favourite haunt of witches. Logan stones are boulders placed so precariously that although they rock when touched they are extremely difficult to actually dislodge. There is a true story of the stone being rocked and eventually dislodged by a naval lieutenant, a nephew of Goldsmith, and twelve of his friends in 1824. The stone rolled from

its perch and landed up on the beach but local protests were such that the perpetrator was forced to spend a small fortune in attempting to have the stone restored to its original position but, it is said, the stone does not rock as freely today as it once did.

In this spectacular place it is not too difficult to visualize witches gathering around the Logan Rock on nights of the full moon, with their potions and cauldrons, and working such magic in their covens that they thought they flew to Wales to drink the lovely fresh milk of Welsh cows. Today the Logan Rock and the enchanting beauty of Porthcurno can still exert a strange power and influence over many people. A mysterious place indeed.

St Ives, Cornwall

The famous beach and bay at St Ives has long been reputed to be haunted; it also has a distinct and unreal atmosphere on occasions.

The phantom bells, the ghost ship and the ghost figures seen at St Ives I have dealt with in my *Ghosts of Cornwall* (Bossiney, 1983) but in April 1986 a fellow-member of the Society for Psychical Research, Mrs Pauline Clare, related a curious interlocking experience at St Ives in a letter published in the Society's Newsletter. I am grateful to Mrs Clare for permission to quote her story here. She writes:

'I am of Cornish descent. On holiday at St Ives during the summer of 1928 as a girl in my early twenties I went down alone to the beach one afternoon. The sand was wet with the falling tide and I wanted to dance. I looked round to see no-one was there and began to do so. A sea mist came on, and presently a boat landed, full of bearded men, who pulled her up over the sand. They obviously did not see me, and though they huddled together talking anxiously I could not hear their voices. The beach seemed to have changed, it was shorter and steeper, and bushes grew there. Presently the men

LEFT: *Mysterious Logan Rock, once the haunt of witches.*

made their way uphill towards a cliff side. I thought they were Romans, who used to come to Cornwall for the tin; not real living people.

'Some years later I met another Cornishwoman, a Mrs Day, and mentioned St Ives to her. She said something odd had happened to her there on holiday as a girl. Sitting with other young people at the top of a cliff she had noticed a group of men clambering up. They had beards and long robes. Once arrived, they formed a circle, kneeling down to reverence one in the middle. A boy beside her asked, "What are you dreaming about?" She said she was watching the funny men. When he said, "What men?", they vanished. She was much teased about it. Until the figures disappeared she had thought them real—film actors perhaps. Later she believed they were Phoenicians.

'I checked that the cliff was the same one that I had seen, and realised that if *my* men had scrambled up it they would have come out just above where she saw them. I wonder whether some Cornish race memory held the picture, or whether the imprint was simply in the place itself.'

In a letter dated 13 August 1987 Mrs Clare tells me: 'I thought it interesting because of the coincidence of Mrs Day seeing the men when they had climbed the cliff. She and I are possibly distantly related. I think the place impressions may be in our genes, handed down through many generations . . . I think the change in the coastline at St Ives is interesting too. I "saw" the slope up from the beach as quite close though actually I was far down the beach and Mrs Day saw the men come up "over the edge of the cliff"; but in the far past it would have been only a slope up from the *then* edge of the tide. The erosion there must have been considerable.'

Mrs Pauline Clare ends her letter: 'I am a born psychic and have seen "ghosts" since babyhood. Both my daughters are psychic but in different ways. The great advantage of psychism is the knowledge that there is no death. I am eighty-two and near the end of this "stage" and eagerly looking forward to getting rid of my worn-out old body, well though it has served me . . .'

RIGHT: *St Ives, about 1900. Ghosts frequented St Ives in such large numbers that a professional ghost layer was employed well into the nineteenth century.*

Wadebridge, Cornwall

A farm here was once a manor house and the story of this haunted spot has been related by, among other people, Arthur H. Norway in his *Highways and Byways in Devon and Cornwall* (Macmillan, 1897)—he calls this delightful area 'a haunted valley'.

One afternoon the farmer had occasion to go into town; his wife accompanied him and there was no-one else at the house. Darkness had fallen by the time they returned home and as they approached the farmhouse across the farmyard they were surprised to see all the shutters open and lights in all the rooms of the house and the sounds of many people inside the property. As they stood and looked they saw what appeared to be unknown people in ancient dress and costume passing to and fro in the various rooms.

Drawing nearer and looking through the window into the main room they were amazed to see a long table set with bottles and decanters such as they had never seen before; and the noise, at close quarters, was overwhelming and disturbing. Shouts, oaths, scraps of obscene songs, bursts of wild laughter and strange curses reached their bewildered ears.

After watching and listening for some little time, the startled couple plucked up their courage and marched up to the front door but the farmer had no sooner put the key into the lock than every light went out and the howls and cries and laughter ceased instantly. The sudden and absolute silence was almost as terrifying as the mysterious sights and sounds had been. Inside the house the puzzled farmer and his wife went from room to room but there was no living person in the house, apart from themselves, and of the wild band of strange people they had seen and heard there was not a single trace.

Another farm in the immediate vicinity has a room where, it is said, if you are left alone in it at night, a small, cold hand is gently placed in yours. Nothing is seen or heard but 'softly, confidingly, as

RIGHT: *Egloshayle Churchyard: '. . . haunted by a ghostly white rabbit.'*

if human warmth were what it sought, this icy little palm steals into yours, and nestles there'. Curiously enough exactly the same is said to happen on occasions in the Prince of Wales Room at Bramshill, Hampshire's most haunted house. There many visitors, without knowing other people have experienced the same thing, have reported feeling a child's invisible hand being placed in their...

In the Wadebridge area the ancient bones of a man were found beneath the flooring of an upper room in an old house; and a slashed doublet and other clothing of the Stuart period; seemingly the evidence of a murder committed more than two centuries ago. The room where the remains were discovered still harbours the ghost of a cavalier as it did before the remains were uncovered. Those who have seen the fearsome figure say the locks of his hair drop over his shoulders, his foppish clothes are colourful but worn and his spurs ring sharply on the old oak floor. He is most commonly seen in the grey light of early morning, the time of day perhaps when he met his untimely death.

Wadebridge also has a haunted hotel where a phantom coach has been seen and heard at midnight on certain nights of the year; a delightful cottage that is or used to be haunted by three ghostly monks; a church haunted by a ghostly white rabbit and the shade of a man who set out to put an end to the phantom animal; while nearby there is an old house where many strange happenings have been reported, and where my wife and I witnessed something of the haunting during the course of a visit; and there is a bridge that is haunted on nights of the full moon . . . but I have written about these two cases elsewhere in my books for Bossiney.

Winkleigh, Devon

Nearby West Chapple Farm was a mysterious place long before the strange three-way agricultural suicide there in September 1975. Divided ownership had made it 'an emotional penitentiary in which each was the jailer, each the jailed' as Robert Robinson put it during the course of his Channel Four television programme in 1987.

The Luxtons had been a prominent family in this district of Devon for many centuries; they inhabited the nearby manor of Holcombe as long ago as the sixteenth century and there are numerous references to them in the records and in the churches of Winkleigh and Brushford Barton.

Fifty years ago the father of the three Luxtons who died opposed the building of the community hall in the centre of the village of Winkleigh; not only was he aware of the story of a ghostly carriage drawn by two headless horses that haunted the vicinity, he was also acutely aware of the curse that would reputedly fall on those who tampered with the ancient knoll where it was proposed to build the hall; perhaps most importantly however he knew, perhaps more than most people, about the secret underground passageway in the mound and what it contained . . . In the event the hall was built, no great calamity occurred to the Luxtons (or at any rate not for half a century) and nothing incriminating came to light from the secret passageway.

The simultaneous deaths of the three residents of West Chapple Farm, 'the farm where time stood still', shocked the whole countryside hereabouts and the local newspapers carried lurid stories about disappointed love affairs and wrangles over property while in hushed whispers the local people talked of incestuous activities, madness in the family, ghosts and hauntings at the farm, and responsibility for the deaths outside the family.

The bodies had been discovered by a butcher who made a regular call at the isolated farm which had somehow managed to escape much of the progress of the twentieth century. There was no mains water or metered electricity although the Luxtons were the first farmers in the locality to have both the 'phone and a car. The farm had been owned and run since the Second World War by two brothers, Robbie, aged 65 at the time of his death, and Alan, 53, together with their sister Frances, aged 68. All three had been born on the farm, as had their father before them. None of the three had ever married; 'nobody was good enough for them' although Alan had been engaged at one time and very much in love it was said. He wanted to sell his share of the farm and move out but his brother and sister would not agree. There were tremendous rows but no solution and in the end Alan ended his engagement. The three of them had lived all their introverted lives at West Chapple Farm and they were all to die there.

The butcher, Jim Reynolds, found the place deserted when he made his routine call but he saw what he took to be a scarecrow lying on an incline near a barn. When he approached the object he was horrified to find it was Alan Luxton, dressed in pyjamas and unlaced boots, lying with arms folded. There was no sign of any weapon although the top of his head was completely missing from below the eyes. Reynolds hurried back to Winkleigh and reported his findings to the police.

Soon the place was bristling with policemen and before long fragments of flesh and bone and portions of human brains were found around the farmhouse, on the lawn and in the overgrown flowerbeds, by the farm gate and towards the orchard. Having ascertained that there was no sign of the dead man's brother and sister in the untidy house the police began a thorough search of the farmyard and immediate vicinity. Soon two more bodies were found, lying side by side in the grass among cider apples in the orchard.

Frances had been wearing a nightgown which was drawn up around her midriff and her body was in a very curious position. She was on her hands and knees, her legs drawn up almost as if in prayer. The top of her head had been blown off and a large section of her brain, practically intact, lay on the ground several feet from the body, almost as though it had popped out of her head. Robbie's body lay alongside, dressed in trousers, a vest and unlaced boots. He too had obviously died from massive head injuries but in addition there were several cuts right through one cheek and about the lips and ears. An old shotgun lay nearby.

At the subsequent inquest it was stated that the injuries to Robbie's face were consistent with having been made by a blunt knife found in the dead man's pocket. At the time it was more or less accepted that Alan had died first, then Frances and finally Robbie, possibly as much as two hours after Alan.

Local people were deeply shocked. The Luxtons were more or less recluses and they had a reputation for meanness but they were regarded as good Christians, although night-time visits to churchyards and muttering and talking to no visible persons in graveyards was something else. Frances it was noted was 'too proud' to go to church at Winkleigh. She went to Brushford where 'she could act the lady of the manor'. Such expressions as 'I'll never understand why they did it' were heard on all sides. Could something out of this world have been responsible? Certainly there were stories of strange goings-on at the isolated farmhouse; loud shouts and screams and long periods of silence; the Luxtons never talked about themselves; and mysterious or even terrifying events that they experienced would be kept to themselves; rather than talk to the world about any difficulties or troubles they would have put an end to themselves first. Is that in fact what happened?

That there were events and stories that have never surfaced is accepted by everyone who has looked into the strange affair at West Chapple. Some of the local people said at the time and still say 'nobody around here will tell you the full story although there are plenty of us know what we know and we're keeping it to ourselves . . .' After the deaths the two brothers were buried with their father

West Chapple Farm, a mysterious place, scene of the three-way agricultural suicide in September 1975.

and mother at Winkleigh but Frances was buried at Brushford. 'Snobbery beyond the grave' commented one Winkleigh resident. 'Always going to church, no matter what they did, no matter how they behaved. We have our own ideas about her and Robbie. It ran in the family, that did. You've never known so much intermarrying, one after the other marrying cousins and aunts and nephews and what have you—and carrying on with each other.'

More than one local family who might be expected to know regarded Alan as less than sane for a good many years; people told me that what they did must have caused 'terrible guilt' and a family with such a history gets cursed. The terrible end that the three Luxtons met was regarded by some as retribution: '. . . wiped off the face of the earth, they were.'

Some people thought that money lay at the root of the Luxton tragedy. The family had been great landowners and very wealthy; then gambling and drinking ran through a lot of money and one of the worst of the family broke his neck after falling from a horse. The grandfather blamed it all on drink, gambling and spending on worldly things; he was determined that nothing would be wasted, nothing and nobody should leave the farm. Marriage for the grandchildren was discouraged in case the wives or husbands should become spendthrifts and squander the farm money. The three doomed children grew up in this atmosphere and as time went by Robbie became worse than his father (which was saying something) and towards the end Frances, it was asserted, was even worse still.

Alan, perhaps because he was ill and violent, perhaps because he wanted to talk, perhaps because he was terrified of what he had heard and seen—whatever the reason, used to be locked up in his room; in a room that Robbie and Frances had specially prepared for him. There were stories of terrible rows and unspeakable happenings. A proportion of local people thought he murdered his brother and sister before committing suicide; they had ruined his life and during the latter days when they wanted to sell-up, Alan refused to co-operate as they had refused to co-operate with his

LEFT: *West Chapple Farm: where 'time stood still'.*

wishes years earlier. Alan rarely left the farm after that deep family disagreement and he never forgave them. He grew to hate women with a callousness and coldness that was truly frightening. Yet the sale of the farm was more or less completed before the deaths. It was an atmosphere ripe for psychic activity.

John Cornwell, staff editor of the *Observer* foreign news service, wrote up the story of the Luxtons and the violent deaths of three members of this ancient Devon family. He entered the deserted house soon after the deaths and found the bed in the master bedroom looking as if it had not been made for ten years with soiled clothing in heaps all over the place; a second room was full of clothes fashionable forty years earlier and a third bedroom was really filthy and full of rags, sacking and piles of rotting newspapers. 'I sensed an atmosphere of bitterness and despair,' he wrote. 'There was an overpowering, evil stench . . .'

Not long before the triple deaths Robbie said, speaking from the depths of wretchedness and misery: 'It's all a mistake; we shouldn't be going.' Frances too came out and said, 'The farm should never have been sold. We should die on the place' and she repeated this prophetic sentence several times.

Towards the end all the three Luxtons at West Chapple Farm became very depressed, practically stopped eating and consequently became very thin; but they remained Luxtons to the end, moody, quick to anger and deeply religious.

At the inquest it was more or less decided that Alan had committed suicide, Robbie and Frances had rushed out and found the body and in their depressed states of mind an hour or so later Frances had 'acquiesced to the actions of the person' who shot her and then Robbie had shot himself. There seems little doubt that in one sense or another, Alan in particular, but probably all three were haunted by the ghost of their father.

Susan Barrett, the playwright and novelist, told John Cornwell that she had come to almost dislike the Luxtons and she found West Chapple 'distinctly creepy', sensing an atmosphere of gloom and evil. On her first visit, she said: 'I wandered around for quite a long time and found it delightful; then suddenly in that garden at the back, where Robbie and Frances killed themselves, the air seemed to go hot against my skin and there was a strange sort of pressure in the atmosphere. I turned and got out as fast as I could; it was like being hounded by the pressure . . .'

The Author in Cornwall.

Even a member of the psychiatric staff at Wonford Hospital, where Alan Luxton was treated for mental illness, has described mid-Devon—the Winkleigh area—as 'a weird place, a place where people can hide, where people can behave in an abnormal fashion without discovery . . . it's a peculiar locality . . . those hidden valleys and high hedges, the secretiveness . . .' It is a landscape of combes and Saxon earthworks, of patterns shaped by prehistoric paths and cattleways, a landscape criss-crossed by mysterious ley-lines. When I was there in the summer of 1987 I met and talked with a number of local people. None of them had anything good to say of any of the Luxtons and several of them were convinced from personal

West Chapple Farm today.

experience that the place was haunted, 'had been for years, before the Luxton affair . . . and always will be . . .'

Today West Chapple Farm is owned by John Gledhill who admitted to John Cornwell that he had 'become rather obsessed with the Luxtons but it doesn't bother me living in a house where there has been a violent tragedy. When I first came to the farm I thought it was beautiful but I found it was absolutely dead. I suppose I was spooked in that sense. Most farms are alive; but something had gone out of West Chapple. The shed with the water wheel completely terrified me. I felt a terrible pressure and I had to get out. At first I thought I could never live in the place . . .'

Select Bibliography

Bizley, Maurice H., *Polperro Twixt Looe and Fowey,* Rickard, n.d.

Bord, Janet and Colin, *Ancient Mysteries of Britain*, Grafton, 1986.

Cornwell, John, *Earth to Earth*, Allan Lane, 1982.

Dewar, H.S.L., *The Giant of Cerne Abbas*, W.C. Folklore, 1968.

Grinsell, Leslie V., *Folklore of Prehistoric Sites in Britain*, David & Charles, 1976.

Legg, Rodney, *Mysterious Dorset*, Dorset Pub. Co., 1987.

Lethbridge, T.C., *The Power of the Pendulum*, Routledge & Kegan Paul, 1976.

Mais, S.P.B., *The Cornish Riviera*, Great Western Railway Co., 1928.

Norway, Arthur H., *Highways and Byways in Devon and Cornwall*, Macmillan, 1897.

Pepper, Elizabeth and Wilcock, John, *Magical and Mystical Sites,* Weidenfeld & Nicolson, 1977.

Underwood, Peter, *The Ghost Hunters*, Robert Hale, 1985.

— — *Ghosts of Cornwall*, Bossiney, 1983.

Westwood, Jennifer, *Albion: A Guide to Legendary Britain*, Grafton, 1985.

Wilcock, John, *A Guide to Occult Britain*, Sidgwick & Jackson, 1976.

Williams, Guy, *A Guide to the Magical Places of England, Wales and Scotland*, Constable, 1987.

Also Available

GHOSTS OF CORNWALL

by Peter Underwood
Peter Underwood, President of the Ghost Club, journeys across haunted Cornwall. Photographs of haunted sites and drawings of ghostly characters all combine to prove that Cornwall is indeed a mystic land.
'Britain's top ghost-hunter . . . fascinating. . . .'

The Sunday Independent

GHOSTS OF DEVON

by Peter Underwood
Peter Underwood, President of the Ghost Club, writes of the ghostly stories that saturate the county of Devon, a land full of mystery and of ghostly lore and legend.'
'Packed with photographs, this is a fascinating book.'

Herald Express

GHOSTS OF SOMERSET

by Peter Underwood
The President of the Ghost Club completes a hat-trick of hauntings for Bossiney.
'. . . ghostly encounters that together make up the rich tapestry of the Ghosts of Somerset.'

Western Gazette

WESTCOUNTRY HAUNTINGS

by Peter Underwood
'The Westcountry offers. . .just about every kind of ghostly manifestation. . .'writes Peter Underwood, president of the Ghost Club. '. . . a chilling look at hauntings from Bristol to Cornwall . . . many of the accounts appear for the first time.'

David Henderson, The Cornish Guardian

MYSTERIES IN THE SOMERSET LANDSCAPE

by Sally Jones
Sally Jones, in her fourth Bossiney title, travels among the Mysteries in the Somerset Landscape. An intriguing journey among deep mysteries in a 'fascinating and varied landscape.'
'This is a whirlwind package holiday of sorcery and legend, touching down here and there before whizzing off in search of still more fascinating fare.'

Mid Somerset Series of Newspapers

SECRET WESTCOUNTRY

by Hilary Wreford, Rosemary Clinch & Michael Williams
'. . .according to Bossiney tradition brilliantly produced, with a fine range of photographs and drawings. Many intriguing a tale is unfolded.'

The Cornish Banner

MYSTERIES IN THE DEVON LANDSCAPE

by Hilary Wreford & Michael Williams

Outstanding photographs and illuminating text about eerie aspects of Devon. Seen on TSW and Channel 4. Author interviews on Devon Air and BBC Radio Devon.

'. . .a fascinating book. But it is worth getting just for the superb pictures. . . .'

Express & Echo

WESTCOUNTRY MYSTERIES

Introduced by Colin Wilson

A team of authors probe mysterious happenings in Somerset, Devon and Cornwall. Drawings and photographs all add to the mysterious content.

'A team of authors have joined forces to re-examine and probe various yarns from the puzzling to the tragic.'

James Belsey, Bristol Evening Post.

PARANORMAL IN THE WESTCOUNTRY

by Michael Williams

'Michael Williams of Bossiney Books has produced another of his well illustrated books of strange goings-on. . . . He explores ghost hunting, healing, psychic painting, tarot cards, mediumship, psycho-expansion, astrology and more.'

Allan Tudor, Herald Express

SUPERNATURAL ADVENTURE

by Michael Williams

Contains a great deal of unpublished material relating to the Supernatural.

'Spiritual healing, automatic writing are just a few of the spectrum of subjects . . . neat, well-presented . . . easy-to-read volume.'

Psychic News

DAPHNE DU MAURIER COUNTRY

by Martyn Shallcross

A special look at Cornwall in which the internationally-famous novelist set important stories.

'A treasure chest for those who love Cornwall and the du Maurier novels.'

Valerie Mitchell, The Packet Group of Newspapers

SUPERSTITION AND FOLKLORE

by Michael Williams

A survey of Westcountry Superstitions: Interviews on the subject and some Cornish and Devon folklore.

'. . . the strictures that we all ignore at our peril. To help us to keep out of trouble, Mr Williams has prepared a comprehensive list.'

Frank Kempe, North Devon Journal-Herald

We shall be pleased to send you our catalogue giving full details of our growing list of titles for Devon, Cornwall, Dorset and Somerset and forthcoming publications.
If you have difficulty in obtaining our titles, write direct to Bossiney Books, Land's End, St Teath, Bodmin, Cornwall.